Date Due

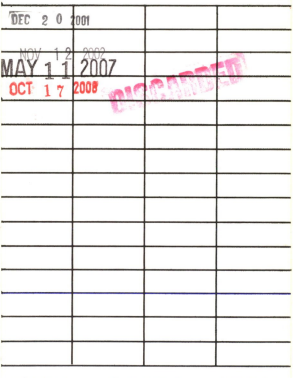

DEC 2 0 2001			
NOV 1 2 2002			
MAY 1 1 2007		DISCARDED	
OCT 1 7 2008			

AUTISM, ART, AND CHILDREN

AUTISM, ART, AND CHILDREN

The Stories We Draw

Julia Kellman

BERGIN & GARVEY
Westport, Connecticut • London

Library of Congress Cataloging-in-Publication Data

Kellman, Julia, 1943–
    Autism, art, and children : the stories we draw / Julia Kellman.
      p. cm.
    Includes bibliographical references and index.
    ISBN 0–89789–735–8 (alk. paper)
      1. Autism in children—Treatment. 2. Art therapy for children. I. Title.
  RJ506.A9K44 2001
  618.92′89820651—dc21   00–064209

British Library Cataloguing in Publication Data is available.

Library of Congress Catalog Card Number: 00–064209
ISBN: 0–89789–735–8

First published in 2001

Bergin & Garvey, 88 Post Road West, Westport, CT 06881
An imprint of Greenwood Publishing Group, Inc.
www.greenwood.com

Printed in the United States of America

The paper used in this book complies with the
Permanent Paper Standard issued by the National
Information Standards Organization (Z39.48–1984).

10 9 8 7 6 5 4 3 2 1

Copyright Acknowledgments

To special artists everywhere

And in memory of Marilyn Zurmuehlen, my mentor and friend

Contents

Figures

Acknowledgments

The many memories of my mentor, the late Marilyn Zurmuehlen, continue to guide both my research and writing, keeping me focused on what is essential to both—good stories and finely crafted, descriptive language. I am certain that without her example as scholar, writer, and artist, I would not be able to think, write, or even inquire as I do. Of course, the many friends who have read my manuscripts, put up with my occasional lunacies, and helped through their kindness and willingness to listen all deserve my thanks—Jo, Patrick, Laura, Fred and Velga, Jim and Karole, Paula, and Terry. My largest debt of gratitude, however, is to my spouse, Phil Miller, for his years of good-humored willingness to endure sandwiches and solitary summers and his unflagging support and enthusiasm for my various projects, and for his always keen eye and sensible advice on images of all sorts. The Dean's Travel Grant, College of Fine and Applied Arts, and The University of Illinois at Urbana-Champaign also made a summer's research considerably easier to accomplish.

1

Introduction and Explanation

Years ago I took an introductory class in cultural anthropology. One particular video from the course still remains fresh in my memory. It featured the Dani people of New Guinea, explored their lifeways, subsistence patterns, and the often hostile interactions with other bands who lived near them by describing their culture from the perspective of an eight- or nine-year-old boy. A seemingly unremarkable incident early in the film struck me as especially significant as the camera panned the lush highland scenery and the gardens of the community. In this sweep of the camera, one sees the boy seated in the tall grass at the far edge of his family's garden, idly drawing in the dirt with a stick as he watches over the pigs feeding in the undergrowth at the edge of the nearby stream. The camera briefly records the marks in the dirt, too, leaving just enough time to decipher the several shapes before it moves on. The scratches appear to form the outline of the all-important Dani garden, the source of most of the people's food, the responsibility of men, the grounding of each family's wealth and social standing. At the side of the image closest to the boy lies a square, certainly the guard tower, and in the center, carefully delineated patches seem to indicate various crops. The entire image is enclosed with a solid line, setting it off from the imagined surrounding gardens and from the uncultivated area near the stream, where the boy himself actually sits with his stick and pigs.

The little dirt drawing is more than simple idle scratching, for as it delineates a garden plot, it also describes the child's future, his major adult occupation, and an image of the heart of his small community. It is a description of a literal place as well, and it surely illustrates a central aspect of the boy's own home in the heart of the New Guinea highlands. For these reasons the boy's drawing can be seen as "the story or narrative in terms of which [his] one's life makes sense" (Bellah, Madsen, Sullivan, Swindler, & Tipton, 1985, p. 81), for without a garden, a Doni male is without hope for the future—without food for his family or appropriately grounded community relationships. In a way, a man without a garden is a man without a country, a man without means to make sense of his life; the boy's drawing tells, in the clearest way possible, the only story in terms of which the boy's life can have meaning in his garden-based world.

This relationship of art (both child and adult), story or narrative, and sense or meaning making has engaged my attention for as long as I can remember, for I myself have always understood the world in terms of stories. Beginning with my adventures with my invisible playmate Milklens and the later ongoing saga of a burgeoning clay mouse community that I constructed in my desk throughout first grade, narrative has elaborated my existence. Long after Milklens left my life, this rodent community described and enacted, in each addition of clay mice and cardboard homes, all the experiences that I then felt were essential for a child both with her parents and with her small social world; I created meaning and sense for myself at the same time that I had Mouse play with her friends, help her family celebrate a holiday together, or let her explore the inside of my desk. I practiced and made concrete tenderness and caring at the same time I told myself my story, tucking Mouse under her tiny candy box quilt at the end of the school day.

Other children tell stories, too, and the stories they create and the art they make to relate those narratives inform us not only of their fantasies and experiences, but also of the deeply significant ongoing stories of their young lives. It is as conveyers and constructors of meaning that narrative and art play their most important roles, for it is through images and words that children inform themselves of how their world is put together, how they must interact with it, and what is of consequence in their lives. We will begin our inquiry here, looking for signs of personal stories in art, listening for the sometimes nearly inaudible sounds, and moving carefully to uncover the various roles of such narratives in the lives of the children who create them.

To advance understanding of how art images may represent personal meaning beyond the clear subject of a text (i.e., the vase of flowers in a still life, the sitter in a portrait), experts who can provide maps for part of the journey need to be consulted and meaning itself needs to be defined. Once that is completed, we can begin our explorations with at least the sure knowledge of which road we must take to get out of town headed in the right direction. We will start with the word "meaning," which includes: having significance, intending, having the purpose; intended to be or in fact is, conveyed, denoted, signified; sense, understanding, knowledge (*Webster's New Twentieth-Century Dictionary*, 1979). Significance appears to be that which one strives to discern in experience to make sense of or to understand the flow of events around them. Without this understanding, the happenings of one's life appear a jumble, unrelated elements arriving and departing to no particular purpose. According to the sociologist Alfred Schutz (1970), meaning is established in retrospect, through interpretation of experience. It is this reflective, backward-looking aspect of meaning making that explains the frequent after-the-fact quality of what we individually encounter; because it is individually constructed, this type of meaning is subjective since it is not an attempt to follow logic-bounded scientific investigatory procedures. This personal significance, or meaning, is clearly a description of our own lived experience; it is the text of our lives. Psychologist Jerome Bruner (1986) clarifies this point further when he writes that meaning and reality are, in the end, interchangeable categories, thus indicating the connection between the ongoing creation of our lives and our stories.

Many people have pointed out that telling a story is an important means to discovering who we are. In Barry Lopez's book *Crow and Weasel* (1990), the title characters are two adolescent boys who finally become adult men after their long and arduous spiritual and geographic quest. The first public thing they are to do when they return home is tell the story of their experience to their community. "[W]e will tell the stories that were given to us. We will share all we have learned," Weasel tells Mountain Lion (p. 60). This storytelling will not only form and strengthen their community's social bonds, but will also provide an opportunity for the young men themselves to reflect on, savor, and continue to interpret their long journey. It is this three-way interaction that helps us devise the very self we encounter in our stories, for through language as well as images, we construct and share our experiences as we describe them in narrative.

For years, Vivian Gussin Paley (1990) taught preschool and kindergarten at the University of Chicago Laboratory School until her retirement in 1997, using storytelling in her classroom to engage her students in just this reciprocal, discovering, and constructing manner. Her students told their stories to one other as a means of discovering themselves and each other within the flow of classroom play. Paley writes, "Play and its necessary core of storytelling are the primary realities in the preschool and kindergarten, and they may well be the prototypes of imaginative behavior throughout our lives" (p. 6). Somewhat later she remarks, "In storytelling a child says, 'This is how I interpret and translate right now something that is on my mind'" (p. 10), thereby describing the individual interpretive, communicative, and creative nature of stories.

Child psychologist Susan Engel (1995) also investigates children's stories and their roles in children's lives. She explores their narratives, explaining that these often short, repetitive, or seemingly simple stories are, in fact, "the real stuff of mental development. The construction, telling, and retelling of stories allow children to learn about their world and reflect on their knowledge. The making of stories also allows them to know themselves; through stories, children construct a self and communicate that self to others" (p. 206). In this way, stories are also a way to reinvent the world, for storytelling, if nothing else, is a creative, fluid undertaking.

Jerome Bruner (1986) adds to our understanding of the use of narratives in his investigations of cognition and the mind in which he describes two modes of thought or knowing, both particular and distinct ways of ordering experience and constructing reality. These two modes are the narrative, which searches for the connections between events to establish verisimilitude, and the paradigmatic, or the logical, scientific mode, which seeks to establish truth through proofs. One attempts to tell a good story, the other to convince one of its truthfulness. Bruner begins his inquiry into these two modes in *Actual Minds, Possible Worlds* with this quotation from William James: "To say that all human thinking is essentially of two kinds—reasoning on the one hand, and narrative, descriptive, contemplative thinking on the other—is to say only what every reader's experience will corroborate" (p. 1). Thus, the separateness of these two modes of thinking is described in still other words, words that state for us in yet another voice the dual nature of the cognitive tools humans usually bring to the task of creating meaning. The mode that is of particular value in our inquiries into children's drawings and their meaning-making, storytelling qualities is, as is clear from its name, the narrative mode, for it is in the flow of events and lived experience that children and art making come together.

The apparent narrative, storylike quality of children's art, along with certain schematic characteristics that adult viewers find particularly ingratiating—"sun" faced, human schema, overall compositions of solidly drawn, designlike forms, baseline-oriented images with stumpy little people, bright golden suns, blue skylines, lollipop trees (with and without holes), blocky dogs with flapping ears, and windmill flowers, for example—have attracted attention to children's art for nearly as long as children have made images in cultures that share Western art-teaching and art-making conventions. The charm of these drawings, and the eagerness of children to share with and explain their contents to adults, have also increased interest in discovering patterns in image production, links between imagery and cognitive functioning and emotional states, and the function of art making in children's development.

The relationship of children's art imagery to narrative is complex. Children may invent, describe, interpret, and negotiate social transactions and personal circumstances and come to terms with their life experiences as they create their art (Kellman, 1995). Children with special needs also reflect in their imagery aspects of their situation, drawing with greater or lesser fine-motor control than their peers, for example, or creating images that appear more or less sophisticated than those of their contemporaries. The intimate connection between the young artist, art, and narrative is an especially fruitful one for both the child and her audience, for it provides the child a means to share her stories with others at the same time she facilitates her own cognitive development (Engel, 1995) in the creation of images that also function in several types of important individual and social transactions.

Harvey the goldfish provides us an example of just such an image, for he allowed his young creator, six-year-old Tania, to express her sorrow, negotiate her coming to terms with circumstances, share her story, and describe in images the various stages of her developing understanding of a difficult situation (Kellman, 1995). On the morning after Harvey's death, Tania used her markers and tempera paints to explore the several problems life had presented her both in the death of her fish and in the death of her father years before. Her first image was a large, frontal view of Harvey in his fishbowl, a bright orange scribble inside a much larger scribble of deep blue that spread across the center of her paper. As she worked, she wondered aloud. What had happened to Harvey? Why did he die? Tania next painted herself holding a pike-sized, shapeless Harvey in her hand as she talked further about her fish. Where had he gone? Who would take care of him? What would become of him now? Her final drawing took some time to complete, and she worked with great concentration with her markers. In this image, Harvey appears as a tiny streak (unlike his previous large scale), just below the rounded, digitless hand of an enormous figure with short-cropped hair and blue trousers. "That's Daddy," she said. "He is watching out for Harvey in heaven. He will help him get used to it" (Kellman, 1995, p. 21).

Tania's worrying, questioning, and, at least for the moment, resolving of difficult life issues form the content of her three drawings. Her bold images allow us not only to share in her love and concern for Harvey and her father, but also to see the record of her construction of her reality, a reality that includes death, loneliness, and a comprehensible and satisfying hereafter. Tania's drawings are, indeed, her "narrative in terms of which her life makes sense."

Another important perspective on Tania's drawings can found in an article by Marilyn Zurmuehlen (1981) in which she investigates intersubjectivity, what Robert Coles explains as "having to do with knowledge and meaning" and the "connection it establishes between meaning and others." She expands this understanding by examining Schutz's discussion of our "'unique bio-graphical situations,'" which are, only in the smallest part, of our own making, for one's private world is an intersubjective one (shared with others), and thus, "'experienced and interpreted'" by them to become "'a world in common to us all'" (p. 24). The world of our daily lives can be understood, therefore, to be an intersubjective one, a world that is interpreted by others. We include their interpretations as part of our experience of them, reshaping the meanings we establish for ourselves to achieve a sense of identity through incorporation of family memories and stories, according to Schutz. Stories of "when I was born," "when I cut baby's hair with the nail scissors," or "when I was little and got lost at the zoo" are some obvious examples of possible familial "interpreta-tion of interpretations," for a child likely does not remember her own birth, or understand an adult's horrified perspective on crude haircuts or feelings other than her own while she was lost at the zoo.

This interpretation, intersubjectivity, and family historicity leads us back to Tania and Harvey, for in her three bold drawings Tania weaves together her family's history (Daddy is dead) with her current life experience (the death of her fish), and applies what she has been told about Daddy (he is in heaven) to solve the painful problem of Harvey. At the same time, her images invite us into her world, to engage in our own acts of interpretation in which Tania's drawings become our own familiar struggles with loss and death as well as the story of a young child's working out difficult life experiences. It is here that personal meaning, community, and the larger social world overlap. As Zurmuehlen points out, "we live in and interpret the world through the mean-ings of our experiences," "taking comfort in the community that is us," in a "world that is common to us all" (1981, p. 26).

Another place to see art used both as a means to express one's individual narrative and to construct coherent personal understanding can be seen in the art of two young artists with autism. Gay Becker's (1997) explanation of cre-ation of narrative in the face of the disruption of disease and disorder in an indi-vidual's life will help us here, for she provides an important perspective on the construction of meaning in narrative terms under difficult circumstances. Becker describes narrative as "the stories that people tell themselves about themselves, reflect[ing] their experience as they see it and as they wish to have others see it" (p. 25). This definition of individual narrative, like Zurmuehlen's, pulls meaning, experience, and stories into ever closer relation-ship, with the need to create meaning from experience providing the core and raison d'etre for the narrative itself. Though Becker examines the narratives of adults, this same linkage certainly also applies to the stories of children, since they, like adults, are faced with the human need to make sense of their lives and the disruptions that shake and shape it. As we will see, this same need to encounter meaning applies to the unique biographical situations of children and adults with autism, for they, more than most, have to struggle to discover meaning and coherence in their worlds and experience.

Jamie and Peter, both young boys with autism, will be our primary exemplars, illustrating with their precocious early drawings many of the characteristics that are most important to our understanding of the relationship of child art images, drawing structure, personal narrative, and the constitution of meaning. Though both boys are unlike their peers in several ways, Victor Lowenfeld (in London, 1997) has pointed out the value of examining even the extreme cases of exceptional young artists, for such inquiries result in clarification of ideas not only about exceptional children, but about other children as well. First we will briefly examine autism. Then we will meet Jamie, then Peter, and uncover what the stories they draw have to tell us about the boys and their attempts to create lives that are grounded in the "world that is common to us all." Finally, we will inquire into what the boys' art making might tell us about other artists—young and old, with and without autism.

For the past several years, I have been particularly interested in studying and documenting the art of children with autism in an anthropological manner, using a phenomenological approach to interpreting data to create case studies that focus on the child as artist, rather than as an example of a handicapping condition. This approach to research and interpretation is somewhat unusual for research about children with autism and their art, for it places the child with autism in the role of a valid artist who is able to develop a visual vocabulary of sustaining narrative images that seem to both create and express meaning for the child and, at the same time, provide insight into the child's world for those who see his or her creations. I have focused on the child's personal, undirected, and drawn individual narratives and stories (with the exception of one image by Peter that I asked him to draw), confident that like another child's complicated use of numbers, clouds, colors, and amounts (Park & Youderian, 1974), emotion is being expressed and meaning created in such acts, and, that like other children, language and image both construct and reflect experience.

Methods used to collect data with the artists described here include: participant observation (drawing, playing, and interacting with children with autism and their families, attending community activities and outings, and sharing meals); review of portfolios; formal and informal interviews with parents, siblings, grandparents, and teachers; review of yearly evaluation records and the current literature for children with autism; and documentation with a tape recorder and camera. Analysis of the data was based on the images themselves and on the children's remarks set within the context of shared experiences, interviews, and art-making sessions. This broad-based, observational research methodology is useful for working with children and young adults with autism, for many cannot talk, and all suffer communicative deficits of one kind or another. Often, direct questioning produces stress in people with autism, and such stress leads to self-abusive, self-stimulating, or tic-like behaviors, making questioning nearly impossible (Frith, 1995). However, since as Schutz (1970) points out, "Knowledge of another's mind is possible through the intermediary of events occurring on or produced by another's body" (p. 164), an interview technique based on sharing time together is possible and valid as well as preferred with many people with autism. At the same time, Schutz's qualitative, phenomenological approach allows researchers to analyze data without quantitative considerations necessarily playing a role, since the researcher's own experience, as Schutz remarks, is as valid a source for interpretation as any other.

This research can be seen as a kind of story, too—the story of encounters with the visual and verbalized narratives of young artists—and these stories serve as both the means and the material of our understanding. This, then, is a story we will create together as we move from classrooms to casual serendipitous encounters, and it will tell an increasingly rich tale of art making as a vital activity for both children and adults. Our story of how art makes meaning, like a river, begins as a rivulet with the stories of two young artists with autism, widens into a stream with the consideration of other children and their art, becomes wider still in the consideration of artists in general, and drops away again into the slender flow of individual lives. Our story will take us to the far reaches of our distant human past and will attempt to explain what we human creatures have been doing as we have marked and shaped our world with the traces and tales of our individual and collective lives.

Artists, Autism, and
a Tale of Structure

I attended the 1995 National Autism Society conference just after school let out for summer break. One of the featured speakers was Temple Grandin, author, professor, designer of livestock confinement systems, and herself a person with autism. The auditorium was packed on the evening of her talk. Parents of children with autism, psychologists, social workers, therapists, and several adults with autism waited impatiently for the appearance of Grandin, who is surely one of the most well-known people with autism in this country, a role model for other people with special needs trying to make their way in an incomprehensible, difficult world. After her arrival, Grandin, a tall, big-boned woman dressed in Levi's, cowboy shirt, and boots, described her life as a person with autism, the long path of both her social and academic learning, and the creation of her thriving confinement design business. The audience hung on every word. Here was a person who could talk about autism from the inside and who, against what seems impossible odds, had developed her special skills and abilities to her best advantage.

"Autistic people often have a talent for drawing," she announced. "They are often visual learners, too, though Asperger [a type of autism] people aren't as often this way. My art was encouraged when I was a child." She flashed slides of several early drawings on the screen, one done when she was seven. None included color. All were of modes of transportation (planes and ships). All employed hasty, sketchy lines, extreme foreshortening, and emphasis on perspective. "I think in pictures," she continued, clicking to images of her current work, drawings of confinement facilities. "I can walk through a plant I am designing in my head. I can't deal with something I can't see or visualize."

The formal qualities of Grandin's drawings are those that I have since come to recognize as being characteristic of much of the imagery of artists with autism. Those wiry electric lines suggest questions that lie at the heart of art making and the special vision and art of some autistic artists. These questions include: Are there similarities in the work of artists with autism? If there are, what does it tell us about such artists and the visual perceptual processes? What might account for such apparent similarities? Brief explanations of autism and the complexities of the vision process itself are important here, for our previous understanding of sociocultural human necessities do not explain how the structure of images becomes the main concern of so many artists with autism, nor do they inform us what such structural interests have to tell us about the way we find meaning and sense in the physical aspects of our world.

Autism, a bewildering syndrome that appears to be genetic in nature or perhaps caused by damage before birth, is part of a long continuum that includes, at one extreme, severely retarded, mute individuals, beset by numerous, compulsive, ticlike behaviors, and at the other, highly articulate, single-minded geniuses with inadequate social skills and a marked inability to take part in the mutual communicative aspects of social existence. Leo Kanner, one of the first researchers to recognize autism, pointed to its main feature, what he referred to as "autistic aloneness," as a description of the mental isolation of an individual with autism. This "aloneness" is often accompanied by intense feelings of anxiety and fear that manifest themselves in angry tantrums (Baron-Cohen, 1995; Wing, 1994). Autism, found in approximately ten out of ten thousand children, with the proportion of boys outnumbering the girls by a ratio of 5:1 at the higher end of the ability range and 3:1 at the lower end, can be diagnosed on the basis of three behaviors (Frith, 1994). These include (1) severe social impairments, defined as the absence of the ability to engage in reciprocal, two-way interactions, especially with peers; (2) severe verbal and nonverbal communication impairment; and (3) absence of imaginative pursuits, including pretend play, with the substitution of repetitive behavior. Uta Frith (1995) identifies the core features of the disorder as the inability to pull together information to create "coherent and meaningful ideas." She explains that there is "a failure in the predisposition of the mind to make sense of the world" (p. 187). The source of these disabilities, according to Simon Baron-Cohen (1995), however, may lie in the fact that people with autism cannot read the relationship of cause and effect in other beings' behaviors, nor do they possess a sense of their own central integrated self, a condition described as "mindblindness." People with autism, according to his view, may be blind to their own and to other people's minds. It is this blindness that leads to the usual severe difficulties in communication, interaction, and imagination. Stephen Mithen (1996), an archaeologist interested in the cognitive development of the human species, has offered a similar explanation for autism, one that also takes into consideration the modular development of the human mind. He proposes that children with autism are born without a mental module for intuitive psychology, that they are unable to take part in the ebb and flow of social relations, though their capacities for intuitive physics, biology, and language remain intact and may even be enhanced. Temple Grandin, from Mithen's view, bears this out in her marked inability to decipher social exchanges between humans and her remarkable empathy and intuitive understanding of animal behavior.

Asperger syndrome, part of the autistic continuum, includes the same characteristics as autism to a greater or lesser degree. These include insistence on sameness, impairment of social interactions, restricted range of interests, poor motor coordination, academic difficulties, and emotional vulnerability (Williams, 1995). However, most individuals with this diagnosis have an average or above average IQ and greater than anticipated language skills. In some cases, language skills are outstanding though they frequently sound pedantic and professorial. Nonetheless, they enable the person with Asperger syndrome to take part in the social world to a far greater degree than most people with autism (Frith, 1994). The ultimate difference, according to Oliver Sacks (1995), lies in the fact that people with Asperger syndrome can tell us of their experiences, inner feelings, and states, and they are able to introspect and report. People with autism are not able to do so.

The lack of pretend play with the substitution of repetitive behavior is of importance to us here, for in its very structure it suggests the first indications of what we may, from our art/image-making point of view, come to understand later as of more interest than simple perseveration. Such repetitive behavior is evidenced in children with autism by the frequent, habitual lining up of toys and other objects, which takes the place of the usual childhood construction of imaginary worlds and adventures. One child, an eighteen-month-old boy, "had a large collection of toy cars, but instead of playing with them in the way of other children, he was interested in placing them in long straight lines and in closely examining their spinning wheels" (Frith, 1995, p. 3). Such children often enjoy rhythmic beating and hitting, forming rows with their toys, or sorting them according to some unfathomable rule. Frequently these objects are part of the child's own collection—matchbooks instead of toys, for example, or whatever else has caught his or her fancy. These idiosyncratic interests and unusual fascinations are exemplified by the rapt attention of a seven-year-old boy with autism described by Frith (1994) who fixated on the specks of fat floating in his soup. The floating fat interested him greatly to move to and fro and to watch, for the changing forms were apparently alive and meaningful to him. However, Frith explains, it is likely a mistake to believe that children with autism have a rich interior life based on their interests, absorption, and repetitive behavior, since these are possibly products of their failure to habituate and on their weakness of control of central thought processes.

Comparison of several precocious artists with autism may suggest additional perspectives on placing, putting, and early mark making, by allowing for the discovery of meaning and purpose in such undertakings. Such a view will enable us to see that it is not necessarily the undifferentiated world with all things of equal import that propels the artist with autism, but perhaps something with which all people struggle, the impulse to create meaning, a shared human necessity.

Five artists each evidencing many of the characteristics of classic autism will serve as our exemplars in our initial inquiries into art by individuals with autism and into the condition of autism itself. These five include Nadia, Stephen Wiltshire, and Richard Wawro, who were, as young children, described as being retarded, with communication problems of greater or lesser severity, social disabilities, and numerous physical and motor problems (Sacks, 1995; Selfe, 1977; Wawro, 1989); ten-year-old Jonathan Lerman, who does not speak (Breen, 1999); and Jessy Park, who was described when she was young as a "high functioning autistic individual," though her autistic characteristics were numerous and her language skills poor (Park, 1982). Jessy, unlike the other four artists, graduated from her local high school. Richard, Jessy, and Stephen developed their art with lessons and classes. Nadia, however, lost her exceptional drawing skill by nine years of age. Nonetheless, all five individuals, difficulties aside, are, or were, artists of astonishing skill and exceptional vision, and for three of them, art has led to public exhibitions, sales, publications, films, and a degree of fame.

We will begin our investigations with Nadia, the little girl whose images still amaze those who encounter them for the first time. Nadia, the child of an immigrant Ukranian family in England, astonished her mother when at the age of three and a half she suddenly displayed an extraordinary drawing ability. This ability in a little girl with no language and who was otherwise functioning at a severely subnormal level continued to develop spontaneously over the next three years (Selfe, 1977). Drawing with a ballpoint pen in sweeping strokes and with great speed and vitality, Nadia produced numerous drawings during her short career, usually of animals and especially of a man on horseback holding a trumpet. These drawings emphasized the outlines, three-dimensional characteristics, and linear qualities of images that she had previously glimpsed in her picture books and included a number of lively sketches of women's legs and shoes. Lorna Selfe (1977), a psychologist who first encountered Nadia when she was six and a half years old, grappled with the many unusual aspects of Nadia and her art making. How did these images arise? How could such a young, differently abled child produce such lively and vivid sketches, which included extreme foreshortening, sure sense of form and three-dimensional structure, vigorous motion, and masterful use of rapid, sketchy line? Were the images eidetic? Was her inability to use language linked in some way to her drawing virtuosity? What did these sketches suggest about Nadia herself?

Selfe followed Nadia's art and development long after the little girl entered a school for children with autism at the age of seven years and seven months. Over time, Nadia became more sociable, enjoying certain group games, learned concepts such as big/little, up/down, open/closed, and learned to obey single-action requests. By the time Nadia reached her ninth birthday, her speech had improved somewhat. However, her drawings no longer displayed her former virtuosity, and her art had become merely the work of a talented child of her own age drawing pictures of teachers and classmates, though periodically, the familiar horse, rider, and trumpet still appeared in the steam on the schoolroom windows (Selfe, 1977). Selfe was led to conclude that the source and motivation for Nadia's art remained enigmatic, though some link might connect her outstanding drawings and simultaneous lack of language skills, and that the precocious drawings served, in Nadia's case at least, as a mark of autism. Nonetheless, other questions remained. How did Nadia draw as she did? What do her drawings tell us about this exceptional artist? And finally, what do her drawings suggest about human capacities? These same questions arise in regard to the art of other artists with autism, and especially in the fresh and precocious drawings of Stephen Wiltshire.

Stephen, son of West Indian immigrants, burst into the English art scene in 1987 as a participant in a BBC special on artistic savants. Since that time, first with his early art teacher Chris Marris, and later under the tutelage of Margaret Hewson, friend, art instructor, and agent, Stephen became increasingly famous, the subject of articles, books, and television productions. His drawings have been published in three books, *Drawings* (1987), *Cities* (1989), and *Floating Cities* (1991); and he has toured Europe, the United States, and Russia. However, despite national attention and acclaim, music lessons to develop budding mime and singing skills, art lessons, school, and diverse interpersonal experiences, Stephen, who would like to be an architect, remains autistic, though he has become an outgoing, friendly individual, and his personal and social growth have been significant (Cole in Wiltshire, 1991).

Stephen's visual preoccupations and talent emerged at the age of five with a fascination with pictures and absorption in the activity of scribbling with paper and pencil; at seven, he showed an obsessive interest in particular images or scenes—buildings, earthquakes, and automobiles. His later highly individual, clearly recognizable style, developed over the years in formal art lessons, displays a keen sense of three–dimensional space, foreshortening, and perspective, all described in vigorous lines and extraordinary detail. This talent of creating visual structure with electric, rapid lines energizes Stephen's numerous drawings of buildings and cityscapes, providing even the most mundane structure with an air of charm and freshness. Despite these capacities, however, Sacks (1995) concludes that Stephen will always need support from others and that "he may never develop, or enter the full estate, the grandeur and misery of being human, of man" (p. 243). Although acknowledging Stephen's outstanding talents, Sacks writes,

> Creativity . . . involves the power to originate, to break away from the existing ways of looking at things, to move freely in the realm of the imagination, to create and recreate worlds fully in one's mind—while supervising all this with a critical inner eye. Creativity has to do with inner life—with the flow of new ideas and strong feelings. Creativity in this sense will probably never be possible for Stephen. But the catching of "thisness"—perceptual genius—is no small gift; it is quite as rare and precious as more intellectual gifts. (1995, pp. 241–242)

It is within the clear-eyed qualities of the art of Stephen and Nadia that their genius as artists lies, and it is this intense and arresting immediacy that we will explore in the following chapter, for these characteristics will connect with the theories of the vision process of David Marr (1982). Marr's theories will, in turn, enhance our understanding of the origin of such bright, artistic exceptionality and vigorous autistic imagery.

Two artists with autism whose art is unlike either Nadia or Stephen's are Richard Wawro and Jessy Park. Their rich paintings sing with color. Jessy divides, controls, and balances her carefully ordered work through repeated hues and linear devices. Richard explores the effects of light within a framework of solid underlying structural elements. Though they, like Nadia and Stephen, focus on the concrete, they paint, not draw, though perhaps one could describe Jessy's paintings as "painted drawings" just as easily, because of their rigid, linear style. Nonetheless, Jessy and Richard create completely realized graphic images that fill their paper from border to border with color as a principal element.

Unlike many people with autism, Richard Wawro, now in his thirties and the eldest son of a Polish-Scottish family, is warm, openly affectionate, and sociable (Wawro, 1989). He first began to draw at the age of three, creating cartoon images when given chalk and a slate by a neighbor. At six, he entered a school for emotionally disturbed children near his home where he was introduced to crayons and paper; his talent for creating charming domestic scenes and children engaged in various activities soon became apparent, surprising family and friends by their display of his graphic skill. By the time he was thirteen, his immense talent was described as an "incredible phenomenon rendered with the precision of a mechanic and the vision of a poet" (Treffert, 1989, p. 89). Richard has continued art making for his own and others' pleasure since that time, specializing in fully realized landscapes in naturalistic, richly blended color built up in layer upon layer of oil crayon (Wawro, 1989). His images, taken from magazine and news photos, compact disc covers, books, or scenes he has briefly glimpsed on television or in the streets of Edinburgh, may appear days or weeks after he has seen them. Though his images are faithful to the original to a degree, Richard always makes a composition his own, changing points of view and including his own particular elements. Firmly drawn dark outlines underlie all Richard's forms, though frequently these lines are obscured by the repeated thick layers of oil crayons he places over them to achieve his shimmering atmospheric effects and intense colors (Wawro, 1989). Only after he has laid out the linear structure does he locate his light source, since light itself is the subject of most of his work (Treffert, 1989). Then, after issues of structure and light have been addressed, he moves on to the rest of the image (Wawro, 1989).

Art is the central interest of Richard's life. He carries his art materials with him everywhere in case he feels the need to begin a painting while he is away from home. In a similarly focused manner, once started he takes a painting to completion though that may not occur for many hours or until the middle of the night. When a painting is finally finished, a family ritual turns its naming and numbering into a shared satisfying and exciting event—a gift of a few pounds to Richard from his father, chanting, hugs—all make painting an exciting as well as a deeply rewarding experience for Richard (Wawro, 1989).

Jessy Park, now in her thirties and the youngest daughter of two American college professors, is a sociable and affectionate individual of average or above-average intelligence, able to work outside the family home and to perform many household chores. Her childhood language skills were poor; however, they have improved somewhat with time. Unlike the other artists we have met, Jessy did not begin making art until high school, when she was introduced to it by a friend and caregiver (Park, 1982). Her mature approach to composition is distinctly her own, however, for she uses solid dark outlines to create her images and, in an almost gridlike manner, orders, structures, and controls the surface of her acrylic paintings with vivid, unnaturalistic, repeated colors, as in her fiercely beautiful painting of the facade of the Duke University chapel. Jessy, like Richard, uses color as an essential element of her art making. Her imagery, taken from photographs or from current obsessions—electric blanket controls, warning and security systems—also springs partially from suggestions made by friends and family members. Jessy also accepts commissions for which she creates paintings of people's homes, utilizing her choice of colors and perspectives as well as one of her longtime interests, the constellations in the night sky (Park, 1982, 1994). However, it is the money that Jessy is paid for each painting and the great pleasure the numbers give her as she adds them to her growing savings account that motivates her to paint at all, for she never makes art without being asked to do so (Park, 1994).

Both Jessy and Richard, the two artists we have seen who emphasize hue, use color in unique ways, each creating rich complex images in easily recognized styles. Jessy employs color as both a subject and as a means of patterning and structuring her images, delighting in colors that are unmodulated, lacking shading or variation in tone. Richard's work is entirely naturalistic; he creates landscapes with subtle color and careful shading as he explores the ever changing properties of light. Nonetheless, Jessy and Richard together share an emphasis on the appearance of the visual world, insistence on that which is concrete, and an underlying engagement with the structure of each image they create.

Our final exemplar, Jonathan Lerman, a ten-year-old American child with autism, will underscore what we have come to see as commonalities among the artists we have examined thus far. The shared characteristics include early and/or sudden onset of image-making abililties, visually based drawing skills, and emphasis on structure as a drawing strategy. Jonathan, like Nadia, began his serious art making suddenly when given charcoal by a young aide at a local community center. Without hesitation, Jonathan began to draw—emotion-packed caricatures, frequently of people he has seen only briefly, made-up characters, or of himself alone in front of a television set or with other characters talking inside his head. Jonathan catches the shapes that constitute his subject's face in his solid energetic line, illustrating in the clearest possible manner the subject's emotional state and creating a recognizable, energy-filled portrait of a moment in time, a flicker of emotion across a human face (Breen, 1999). This use of the linear description of a single instant in such an energetic manner connects Jonathan to the other artists we have seen, for the same acute visual skills and visual memory, and the ability to engage and describe structure with the use of line links him firmly to the art of Stephen and Nadia and in a less obvious manner to the solid, structurally emphatic compositions of Jessy and Richard.

As one might expect, like all artists and individuals, Richard, Jessy, Nadia, Stephen, and Jonathan each demonstrate different levels of art-making skill, interest, motivation, and development. The significant point is not that there is individual variation. It is that the immediate, structural, linear, perspectival qualities of these artists' work, glimpsed at such an early age in several cases, indicate that some similar cognitive process may be taking place in all of them, and that the individual repetitions of subject matter, hues, and forms move far beyond the world of reflexive placing and perseveration to the creation of meaning through richly narrative visual images. The presence and exceptional nature of these five artists' drawings and paintings can be seen to grow out of single, bright visual moments—moments made longer and more accessible to them by autism for, as Baron-Cohen (1995, p. 82) surmises, their world is likely "largely dominated by current perceptions and sensations." If this is so, it is a world less rooted in sociocultural dictates and a personal self-regarding consciousness, more open to a vivid sense of "now." Unlike nonautistic artists whose vision becomes shaded by the confusions of conceptual thinking at the very instant that they recognize an object, artists with autism are likely afforded a clearer view of the visual world because of their less intrusive ability to conceptualize. This explanation of the source of these artists' "unconceptualized view of the world" (Sacks, 1995, p. 243), would neither explain away nor belittle their creations. It would simply suggest a means and direction for elaborating the understanding of artists with autism and the particular characteristics of their image making. This sense of immediacy, this vivid now, brings us to the next portion of our inquiry, for it is this sense of the moment and the vigorous lines used to render it that leads directly to a discussion of the way we see and the manner in which we describe our world both as artists and as visual creatures, as complex beings who think, to greater or lesser degrees, in images and other symbolic notations.

3

Art's Eye, Art's Mind

The cheerful young man in red shorts and white shirt was a regular participant at the new center for adults with pervasive developmental disorders. Born with moderate to severe retardation, cerebral palsy, and autism, he, like most of the other people who attended the center, spent the day taking part in various activities that included field trips, discussion groups, holiday celebrations, music, art, snacks, and lunch. The day I visited the center, art class consisted of either drawing or stringing beads, depending on the individual participant's capacities and preferences. The young man in red shorts was eager to draw. He immediately seized a crayon from the brown plastic basket on the worktable in front of him, and, as if grasping a stick in his fist, bore down on his full-sized sheet of newsprint with such force that it broke with a sharp snap. Enjoying the popping sound made by the crayon as it broke into pieces, he took another. It too, shattered as he dug it into the paper. Encouraged by the art therapist to use the crayon to make marks, not noise, the young man helped himself to a third crayon, red this time, and without seeming to look at either it or his paper, drew a zigzag line in the center of his newsprint, moving from right to left without a pause. The peaks and valleys of this energetic shape were of the same size, forming a solid graphic demarcation of the central horizontal area of the otherwise blank sheet. Taking another piece of paper, and again without seeming to look anywhere but the far wall of the little art room, he repeated the central, horizontal, zigzag form, wriggling with pleasure as he created another identical drawing.

This image certainly was an intentional one, for it was centered, evenly formed, and repeated on several sheets of paper. Though it may have been influenced by the artist's physiological problems that hindered and/or played a role in both his motor control and actions, the image nonetheless required hand-eye coordination and personal preference to create its central, horizontal placement and careful zigzag form. The young man seemed pleased with his drawings, repeating his image as long as the art session lasted, apparently delighting in the kinesthetic motion, the satisfying, repeatable, visual outcome, and his own ability to make marks.

This demarcation of a dominant image and the repetition of particular forms can be found in the imagery of other people, too, as they respond to a drawing surface and create personally satisfying, singular images. Children as young as two years of age make zigzag lines as one of their twenty basic scribble patterns, and they, too, engage in careful placement of marks on paper or other surfaces to form patterns (Kellogg, 1970). Adult artists develop similar compositional strategies and repeated forms in many cultures from the very earliest beginnings of modern human prehistory. Clearly, such images have a particular richness and resonance for both artists and viewers, or why else would they appear with such regularity in so many places, over thousands of years, and in so many widely differing manifestations? How might meaning and narrative enter into this seemingly unadorned engagement with form and structure? How does this simple iconic form fit with the complex art images created by the other artists with autism whom we have seen thus far—artists whose drawings and paintings are rich with details and based on structure? And what, if anything, might these questions suggest about human visual abilities in general and art making and viewing particularly both for people with autism and those without?

To uncover the answers to these and related questions, it is important to consider short descriptions of the processes that make up human vision, the visual/cognitive activities that produce art, the likely roots of the mechanics of art making itself, and visual thinking, since these topics are all bound tightly together like the straws in a broom.

THE SEEING OF ART

Vision, a complex process that is still being explored, engages a full half of our brain's capacity (Hoffman, 1998); it enables us to create the world we see in an immediate and useful manner, describing the physical world and enabling action. Neurobiologist David Marr (1982) provides a useful explanation for the important, early, unconscious portion of our visual processes and also suggests the possible origins of many of the extraordinary abilities of artists and other visual thinkers, both those with and those without autism. Before his death from leukemia in 1979, Marr managed to complete *Vision, a Computational Investigation into the Human Representation and Processing of Visual Information* (1982), in which he explained his approach to vision based on the premise that one cannot understand the act of seeing without first understanding the information-processing tasks being solved by this process. Though Marr presents his work as a series of hypotheses, these hypotheses continue to be borne out by investigations into issues of artificial intelligence, vision, and neurobiology (Sacks, 1985; Crick, 1995; Kass, 1995; Damasio, 1995). Additionally, to the visually sensitive and attentive nonspecialist, Marr's work can be seen to successfully explain many of the puzzling characteristics found in our daily engagement with the visual world. As Marr's work has moved into the mainstream of investigations in perception, his computational theory of visual perception also starts to shed light on art making and artists' use of their own visual processes. Marr's theory also seems to illuminate the particular characteristics of the art of differently abled individuals, notably those with autism.

To become familiar with Marr's central hypothesis and its implications for the artist, and especially the artists with autism we met in the last chapter, a brief discussion of vision and Marr's ideas concerning seeing is in order. According to Marr, it is from the examination of the process of vision and the inquiry into the brain's representations of this information that an understanding of seeing itself will develop. All the wonder, richness, and color of the world appears effortlessly to our eyes. Marr explains that this complex activity of seeing and identifying takes place in less than half a second. For what would it avail someone to see a hurtling bicycle a second too late to avoid it, or to recognize a friend after she has left the room?

According to Marr, evolution favors getting processes started as soon as possible. This is to allow one to avoid danger, seize opportunities for food, shelter, and sociability, and to allow one to locate one's self in an appropriate and useful way in the world. This necessity for speed and for rapidly locating objects in space provides the constraints for the vision process. Additionally, to facilitate this rapidity and to enhance performance as a useful, timely descriptor of what is present in the world, the process of vision itself must remain simple to facilitate both its speed and its ease of operation. The visual process, so essential to comfortable and successful activity, and one that provides food, safety, and ability to be in the visual world, is protected from degradation or loss (as are many other systems) by its structure, i.e., the manner in which it is put together. This visual process structure is modular in nature, thereby providing it a form in which its various functions are separate from one another. In this way, if one portion of the process is damaged through accident or illness, the remaining parts, or modules, can continue to function in a normal way, allowing one to continue to meet one's needs. Since everyone's visual process is modular and everyone must see the world in a seamless manner to be effective, the early modules of the process, what Marr calls collectively the preattentive process, operate in the initial two stages and in the greater part of the third, without one's conscious awareness or ability to control them, like other automatic physical processes or bodily functions. Nonetheless, it is likely that some individuals have a brain that emphasizes particular aspects of their vision process because of innate capacities or variations in a manner similar to the way in which some people have perfect pitch, great sensitivity to touch, excellent fine-motor skills, or a sensitive digestive system. These variations may well spell part of the difference between one artist's vision and another's and a baseball player's eye and a printmaker's.

Since the brain is not a library of perfectly preserved color slides, several things must occur before one can identify an object in the visual world, according to Marr. This can be ascertained by closing one's eyes. At this point, the scene before one is in short-term, immediate memory, yet, the brightness, detail, and complexity fall away, leaving in their stead a simplified, less elaborate version to be recalled. Clearly, there are no bright color slides here to be examined, no intensity to be seen inside one's brain. Marr explains this dilution of the image as the difference between the outcome of preattentive vision—that part of the vision process that occurs an instant before one's brain finishes adding color to its representation, identifying what is before the eyes, and moves to conceptual considerations—and the stored, simplified descriptions of an object. It is this preattentive vision—what one's vision process constructs up to and including the time one begins to recognize an object—that Marr investigates and describes. It is this preattentive vision that appears to form the basis for particular types of image making found in the art of several well-known painters and sculptors and in the art of some autistic artists, whose creations reflect a superb skill in an otherwise retarded or developmentally delayed individual. The following description will help clarify Marr's hypothesis concerning the construction or composition of the perception of recognizable objects.

A brown rabbit grazes on clover in the middle of a grassy yard. Before I think "rabbit," however, this is what occurs, according to Marr. My eyes fall on the scene. Seeing, the end product of this biological process, will begin only after my brain runs the vision process as fast as possible to determine if immediate action is necessary. First, without my conscious awareness, my vision process begins to construct in my brain the image as intensities in a primal sketch, a two-dimensional image based on place tokens or markers that make explicit the amount and disposition of intensity changes in the scene before me. The sketch includes raw (unmodulated) intensity changes and their local geometric structure, zero crossings (the point at which a function's value changes its sign—positive/negative, on/off, black/white, and so on), and other, more complicated groupings and alignments. My brain reconstructs the scene on the basis of these simple markers, which reflect the organization, intensity, and outline of the images that are not yet consciously known to me as tree, grass, and rabbit. All objects are seen as outlines with indications of the amounts and distribution of surface characteristics; the linear outline qualities are particularly significant, since the art of drawing rests directly on just these characteristics.

Next, expanding from and building on the primal sketch, the two-and-a-half-dimensional sketch develops, a viewer-centered representation of depth and surface orientation that deals with shape from motion, stereopsis, and contours. This allows the construction of a depth map of the rabbit, grass, and tree. There is no conscious awareness or recognition of the rabbit nibbling clover. My brain begins to orient the scene spatially, each object assuming a clearer internal form, a distinctive relationship to the whole, and a definite location in space. I still am not conscious of what I am seeing. The scene is not yet in color. This leads to the next phase, the 3–D model, which is an object-centered description, in this case a rabbit-centered representation for shape, computed by my brain. It includes volumetric primitives or elementary units of shape information available in the representation itself. These primitives are arranged in a hierarchical, modular way. The 3–D model allows for recognition of objects by shape, making possible evaluation and action. Using these mental representations based on axes (rather like stick figures) and the generalized cone (a surface created by moving a cross-section along an axis), my visual process resolves the shapes before me. The rabbit becomes a clear, three-dimensional form with recognizable attributes and a specific location on the lawn. Even the direction and speed it is hopping are now certain. Now color is added to the representation (a relative characteristic, dependent on surrounding hues and illumination) and the image is evoked by comparing this particular representation (the rabbit) with stored descriptions in my brain that are associated with my further knowledge (feeding rabbits, warm fur, twitchy noses, and so on). At this juncture my brain begins to compare these descriptions (information and associations with rabbits) and I become conscious of the creature before me. Less than half a second has elapsed. Now I can think, "There is a rabbit, a wild brown rabbit, in the yard, eating clover." This rich, descriptive image is what is available at the pure perceptual level, according to Marr. It is during this initial moment of recognition that the vision process provides the breathtaking clarity and intensity in the act of looking at the world, and Marr believes it is most closely related to the three-dimensional model description. It is at this point that I add conceptual information and can think, "The rabbit must have been born this spring, since it is small." It is this early vision that plays a central role in art making with the observed world as its source.

In regard to artists and art making, Marr's commentary is brief, since his research focused on other issues. Nonetheless, what his work suggests may be of value both for extending our ideas of what it means to see and for enlarging our understanding of artists both with and without autism and their own particular use of vision.

Henry Moore is the first artist that Marr names specifically. As part of the discussion of the 3–D model sketch, Marr describes several of the features of this process, notably, that it provides us with the ability to recognize faces (by utilizing the 3–D model's description of symmetry and verticality) and that the primitives of the 3–D model's representation includes surface primitives of roughly two kinds. These primitives provide the ability to discern "rough, two-dimensional rectangular surfaces of various sizes, including elliptical shapes and circular ones" and that an object is not solid but hollow, a tube or cup, for example (p. 310). In regard to this elaboration of form through surface recognition, he remarks, "Not very many primitives would be needed by the average man, although presumably a sculptor like Henry Moore has a repertoire of hundreds" (p. 310).

Marr, illustrating the possible relationship of the stages in preattentive vision and art, names artists and groups of artists whose work illustrates the careful and frequent disruption of one of the stages of the early vision process. The pointillists, according to Marr, primarily tamper with the image, leaving the rest of the scheme intact. In other words, the pointillists engage in disrupting the two-and-a-half dimensional sketch, which provides information on depth and visible surfaces. In a similar manner, Marr points out that Picasso and the other cubists engage in manipulating the 3–D model image, fracturing and shifting planes, space, and form. Marr concludes that Cezanne, with his astigmatic style, provides a good example of an artist who exploits and utilizes the surface representation or primal sketch stage.

These references to artists suggest a close relationship of preattentive or preconceptual vision and art. Further examination of this relationship indicates that artistically useful attributes of preattentive vision may include the determination of structure and location, arrangements and relationship in space and directionality, the construction of both clear and sketchy outlines and contour images, and the use of foreshortening and perspective. Some artists may have the ability to employ preattentive vision directly in their art making, and in their case the rapidity of preattentive vision processing does not interfere with the artist's possibilities. Art based on early vision displays particular characteristics revealing its origins. For example, color plays a limited role in preattentive vision and is often, though not always, cursory, secondary, or not present. Art that exploits early vision emphasizes the process's attributes in regard to the structure, location in space, and directionality of objects, all of which characterize early vision processes. Freshness, immediacy, and clarity are present to an unusual degree. These and other individual attributes and possibilities lead to the proposition that a relationship might exist between art, artist, and preattentive vision, and provide a grounding for understanding when, how, and why this relationship makes itself known in the creations of various individuals.

The complex relationship of art, artist, and preattentive vision may also play a role in the art of gifted individuals with autism, since they, too, engage in the triangulated relationship of object, visual processing, and image making. What is of interest here, however, is that Marr's insights into this triadic relationship may provide a solid basis for an understanding of the precocity, clarity, and source of the expression of the special visions of the artist with autism.

For the first step in understanding how this triadic relationship might show itself in the art of the artist with autism, it is important to clarify what special physiological predispositions might enable such individuals to take advantage of early visual processing in their work. The second step is to identify what part of such an artist's image making is most likely based on preattentive vision.

These similar visual attributes and abilities may have their genesis in the preattentive vision process itself. This is not to speculate on which portion of the preattentive vision process may or may not be dominant (if such is the case), but to point out that the characteristics of foreshortening, perspective, immediacy, and emphatic linearity as well as the use of black and white imagery may well be explained by their unusual access to a portion of the vision process that is outside the reach of most young artists in any consistent manner. It is to be understood that people with autism are individuals. What is to be considered is that the similarities of their drawing structures and compositions indicate something about their physiology as people with autism.

At this point it is possible to see a connection between Marr's hypothesis of preattentive vision and many of the unusual characteristics found in the creations of artists with autism. The perceptual intensity of preattentive vision process before conceptualization is complete that Marr describes, that instant at the onset of personal pondering and overlays of cultural meaning, may well be the source of autistic imagery and the likely explanation of the intensity and unconceptual nature of their art. At the same time, it is the visual acuity of artists with autism and the resulting ability to apprehend structure and the relationship of forms to one another in three-dimensional space, that provides a connection with other artists with similar abilities in seeing motion, mass, speed, line, and location. And it is this emphasis on visual structure in relationship to the viewer that provides a connection with all other visual thinkers who use their eyes and spatial sense to create and organize their world.

Psychologist Richard Latto (1995) carries his considerations of the role of visual processes in artists' imagery considerably further than Marr. He describes the manner in which our visual systems have developed to analyze the world we inhabit and investigates the means by which artists and viewers alike utilize the way they envision the world to either create or to view art. This is significant information, specially for those artists with autism who use the visual world they inhabit as the subject of their art, for it suggests additional means of exploring the nature of precocious drawing skill and hints at a possible explanation for its appearance in the first place. One of the most immediately useful concepts described by Latto is that of the aesthetic primitive, a satisfying visual form effective because it relates to the properties of the human visual system. According to Latto, such a form is intrinsically interesting, even in the absence of narrative meaning, because it resonates with the mechanisms of the visual system processing it (although I would suggest that the artist's sentience, present in the form itself, is a type of narrative). Some of these forms are universal since they are genetic, and others are culturally determined and must be learned. It is to the universal concepts that we will pay most attention here, for a young artist with autism (Nadia, for example) has not usually learned, and may never learn, the culturally grounded concepts that would influence early, precocious image making. The use and function of line will be our starting point, since line plays a critical role in art.

Artists, both those with and those without autism, and many nonartists as well frequently use line as an element in creative activities and in general mark making. In drawing, for example, edges of all sorts are carefully described in ink, pencil, paint, craypas, charcoal, chalk, and other materials; or lines can be traced in steam or frost, or in sand or dirt, or whatever else comes readily to hand. Lines can be used to form animals, plants, people, and innumerable geometric and nongeometric shapes, all easily observable to viewers who encounter them later in museums and books, on buildings and sidewalks, or on any other surface that can support them. In the visible world of daily experience such marks are frequently the result of human activity, for most objects' edges are not enclosed in literal lines, and the description of forms in nature is not usually carried out in such a specific manner. The curve of a cheek, the folds of a blossom, a soaring rock face elaborated by layers of stone, are not set off from the rest of the world by an actual solid line. There is simply the cheek itself, the flower, the cliff, all physically present, all with visible limits, all embedded in space and time, and all described by our visual system's process of lateral inhibition, our edge detector. The many descriptive lines of this nature are only repeating certain aspects of human visual processing (Latto, 1995). Line drawings like Stephen Wiltshire's buildings are, for example, the outcome of these properties of the visual system to first perceive and then to render images with line. It is this visual process that makes it possible for the artist to draw what she sees by indicating the edges of an object with a line on her paper or canvas. It is this activity of the visual system that allows viewers to respond to such line drawings with understanding and pleasure.

Other constructions that indicate line's importance in human visual process include neural detectors that respond specifically to visual horizontal and vertical orientation and the frequency of lines seen in migraines, illusions of linear fortifications generated as coronas or halos emanating from other migraine-produced images (Latto, 1995). Perhaps a confirmation of the vision system's use of line is also illustrated by the boy in red shorts, whose zigzags clearly were not based on what he saw in his immediate environment. He was likely creating "one of the most important groups of esthetic primitives," a group that includes the boy's zigzag, as well as stripes and other linear patterns that can be found in decorative and fine art throughout the world (Latto, 1995, p. 79). Perhaps, similarly, the excited response of a middle school boy with autism whenever he saw orange and white striped plastic construction barrels was evidence of his pleasure in the stripes themselves, since stripes are an aesthetic primitive, too. It is not too farfetched to presume that the boy with the zigzag and the boy with the stripes might be understood to take delight in the visual stimulation to be found in their preferred forms—simple linear aesthetic primitives, rewarding by their nature, and found in the human visual system itself.

Latto describes several other aspects of visual processing that play a role in the complex creation of art. These qualities account for familiar art categories that include such diverse approaches as landscape painting, portraits and genre scenes, and abstraction. The first of these components critical to art making and viewing is the presence of three channels for processing—one for form, one for color, and one for movement and stereo depth—each category being processed differently. Additionally, these channels are not necessarily more than loosely synchronized, at least in art. The second feature that artists frequently exploit is that visual perception is almost certainly a set of nested modules—color, form/shape, movement, size and spatial frequency, depth, and spatial organization. The third valuable art-related element is that there is a portion of high-level visual processing that responds to the human body, in whole and part—faces, hands, posture, and movement. The fourth aspect that plays a powerful role in art making is the mechanism of fine tuning high-level visual processing to landscape. And finally, the fifth constituent of visual processing of special significance to artists is that of computational modeling and simplification of form as suggested by Marr in his stick figure hypothesis (Latto, 1995). These various operations make it possible for humans to do many things: to recognize the particular place they live and to love landscape painting; to watch and read a human face, body, and hands and to enjoy figure drawing; to observe colors separate from forms and to take pleasure in abstract images in painting and the hues in a sunset; to recognize stick figures and other simplified forms and to understand the perspective described by their orientation and to make sense of Giacometti and his linear sculptural descriptions of the human condition (Latto, 1995). This simple list of visual processing characterisics also seems to suggest additional explanations for the mechanics of art making and viewing as well as the virtuoso performances of young artists with autism whose art has been seen in the past as a "splinter skill" and/or as the creation of an "idiot savant." A more useful understanding of art making by people with autism is that like all artists, artists with autism utilize their visual processes to create "[a]rt [that] defines our humanity by portraying the brain's representation of the world" (Latto, 1995, p. 91) as well as expressing in iconic images or complex imagery their own personal engagement with the universe, the narrative of their lives.

Sylvia Fein (1993) tackles the importance of particular ubiquitous visual forms from another perspective in her examination of the similar shapes encountered in children's early images, prehistoric drawings on rocks, portable objects, and rock shelter walls, and in the art of modern adult artists. Her less biological perspective is useful to us here, too, for it brings us back to the texture of actual image-making experience at the same time she adds support to the more complicated understanding we are developing about the visual process. According to Fein, we have not seriously considered that children and our ancestors "[f]ollow an identical logic, the fact . . . that all of them everywhere on earth discover the same structures which then evolve in subtlety and complexity in the same way" (p. xiii). She explores various forms—circles, spirals, grids, meanders, double spirals, concentric arcs, and others—as they appear in various cultures and in children's art, contrasting the structures by comparing attributes. For example, in the forms of animals with their similar physical structures she points out that many artists—including children, indigenous people from around the world, and prehistoric artists—have all created such creatures by "[s]electing from the structures at their disposal the clearest way to manifest identifying characteristics of the subject, including that which is not visible but vital" (p. 112). The human pleasure in invention and in the creative use of line, texture, simplified shape, and shrewd manipulations of figures and ground is evident in the work of our ancestors as well as contemporary artists; children, too, relish the strength and complexity of such qualities in their own creations. Fein concludes, much like Latto did, that it is in the objects of the human-made world that we see the "[h]uman mind and its ability to express relationships of forms, a unique human birthright" (p. 137).

THINKING IN PICTURES

Temple Grandin (1995b) suggests another important aspect of the "brain's representations of the world" and the "human mind's ability to express relationships of forms"—what she calls "thinking in pictures." She describes her own acute visual processes and her particular ability to employ visualization as a means of concretizing events, concepts, and philosophical considerations, an outstanding characteristic of many people with autism, she suggests. Grandin explains, "One of the most profound mysteries of autism has been the remarkable ability of most autistic people to excel at visual spatial skills while performing so poorly on verbal skills. When I was a child and teenager, I thought everyone thought in pictures" (pp. 19–20). Her description of her thought processes is instructive, particularly in the light of similar abilities apparent in the art of other people with autism. Grandin states, "When I do an equipment simulation in my imagination or work on an engineering problem, it is like seeing a videotape in my mind. I can view it from any angle, placing myself above or below the equipment and rotating it at the same time" (p. 21). She continues, "I create new images all the time by taking many little parts of images I have in the video library of my imagination and piecing them together. I have video memories of every item I've ever worked with" (p. 21). Most significantly, Grandin reports that personal relationships themselves "made absolutely no sense to me until I developed visual symbols of doors and windows" with which to visualize the give and take of social interaction (p. 34).

The many livestock facilities she has designed bring together all of Grandin's various skills, lifelong interests, and personal abilities, twisting them into a long strand of personal narrative, for it is within these structures that she finds meaning for her life that honors the best within her and utilizes her considerable skills. Her acute visual memory, her ability to "think in pictures" is what links Grandin to other people, both artists and nonartists who, to a greater or lesser degree, understand the world in images, forms, and visual relationships rather than in logico-scientific arrangements.

Leonardo da Vinci, a virtuoso artist from childhood, fits into this category, too, with his bird's-eye view of the Arno River Basin in Tuscany and his studies of water currents, which show similar highly developed visual thinking abilities. He was able, because of his exceptional visual skills, to hover in his mind's eye over the entire drainage area of the river and to isolate the many patterns in a wave. Visual thinking skills, deeply entangled with the process of seeing as well as cognition itself, surely must be a significant part of our early human heritage as well, for visual thinking abilities certainly underlie the very first images created more than 32,000 years before the present with collective purpose and group sociocultural learning as well as the artists' own meaning and narrative sense.

To reach our goal of developing an understanding of the relationship of child art images, drawing structures, personal narrative, and the constitution of meaning, especially in the art of precocious artists with autism, we need to digress again, this time for a brief discussion of the interplay of imagery, language, and memory and the role of narrative in people's lives.

THE LANGUAGE PARALLAX AND THE FORMS OF MEMORY

Narrative, the ordering of events or experiences into a structure that contains past, present, and future, carries with it the sense of many things—a story, a shared discourse, a means of personal or group meaning making, a way to arrange in a comprehensible manner the events of one's life. We have seen that visual images (one way of relating narrative), and visual thinking do not necessarily require language to impart meaning. However, the intuitive link of words and images, illustrated in picture books (in which the story, first told in images, can be retold in words), in teaching images (in which concepts are encoded in shapes), and in maps, charts, news photos, and films, all suggest that image and language must surely share some vital aspects of our minds and memories. A journey marked on a map recalls scenes of its progress and places. A single photo explains the horror and dismay of a dreadful event. A film uses our minds as its stage, the action taking place inside our brains as much as on a screen. Later, words can recall these same images to mind. "Did you see? Do you remember?" we say to one another, and we are similarly and simultaneously struck by our recollection of visual shapes and forms of remembered events, places, and experiences.

This recall of events, places, and times gone by, stored in images and externalized in art or language and shared or not as the rememberer chooses, brings us to a discussion of what we have suspected for so long regarding the complex relationship between language, vision, and memory. The interplay between these abilities has begun to take concrete form in the work of researchers using current methods of investigation. Clear linkage between language and interior visual imagery (Kosslyn, Thompson, Kim, & Alpert, 1995) as well as the certain interplay of touch, sight, and language in one small portion of the brain (Büchel, Price, & Friston, 1998) not only suggest an actual connection between internal knowledge and arbitrary symbols, but may also demonstrate the close association of imagery, language, and sociocultural

learning, as well as provide a means to understand the encapsulation of meaning in purely conceptual constructs. Self-reflective autobiographical memories, made up of images of experiences of vivid personal impact, are likely part
of this picture, too, for they maintain the connections of a person's internal
knowledge with the external stimuli in the life-world (Conway, 1990). Such
autobiographical memories suggest a possible linkage between image making
and the expressiveness of art. It is in memory that inner and outer events come
together in recalled forms to create personal meaning that includes a past as
well as a present, a social world of continuing relationships, and a "shared past
which can be remembered and discussed" (Conway, p. 102). In this way,
memory "serves as an important base for the development of private introspec-
tion and the representation of belief systems" (p. 103), as well as provides a
sense of immediacy in the more clearly recalled flow of current events. In this
manner, at least, it seems our memories' images function as midwives at the
birth of our individual interwoven public and private narratives, and it is the
overlap of our inner and outer lives that finds expression in art.

Researcher and experienced elementary teacher Ruth Hubbard (1989)
offers further insights into the interplay of language, visual imagery, and the
creation of personal sense. She explains that images are, at any age "part of
the serious business of making meaning—partners with words for communi-
cating our inner designs" (p. 157). Visual thinking is as important an aspect
of human cognition as verbal skills and is as likely hardwired and prepro-
grammed a component of the total array of human capacities as language itself, according to Hubbard. Internal imagery is a significant aspect of basic
mental forms, for "'the ability to construct and act upon mental representation is regarded as the most fundamental property of cognition'" (Kauffman
in Hubbard, p. 5). For Hubbard, then, our perceptions are the product of
seeing the present with stored images of the past to create meaning. Julian
Gross and Harlene Hayne (1998) add to our inquiry into the connection between language, imagery, and memory, for they point out that if young children are allowed to tell and draw their past experiences at the same time, they
are better able to recall, organize, and talk about the past than if they use only
words to describe their experiences. Therefore, even to recall what has happened in a coherent and useful manner and to sustain one's self as a child situated in time with experiences that mean something is dependent, to a great
extent, on pictorial representation and the rich physiologically based interaction of language and visual imagery.

Psychologist Rudolf Arnheim remarked on this same interdependence of
language, imagery, and meaning when he wrote, "Truly productive thinking is
whatever takes place in the realm of imagery . . . In order to think about objects
and events they must be available to the mind in some way . . . that verbal

thought—words alone—is secondary to shaping thought" (in Hubbard, 1989, p. 5). It is easier now to be certain why such a thing might be the case, for we understand that visual imagery is not merely a prelinguistic undertaking; it is part of the actual mechanics of human language and cognition itself, and it is part and parcel of the meanings we construct for ourselves within the privacy of our minds or in the complicated flow of our social relations. Vivid visual imagery knits together the interior and exterior, past and present experiences of our lives. The art needs of a child or adult with or without autism, as creator or engaged observer discovering order through visible means, should not surprise us, considering the cognitive role of visual thinking. Nor should we find it unusual that drawing and/or viewing images support individual and social memory as well as impart meaning. Before the time of brain scans, Langer (1953) described this for us when she wrote, "Life is incoherent unless we give it form" (p. 400). She further explained that art gives us forms of imagination and forms of feeling at the same time, thereby making meaningful the disparate events of our various worlds. Temple Grandin, Leonardo da Vinci, and the large number of other people, artists and nonartists alike for whom the world is best understood in relationship to visual properties and thinking skills, would likely recognize these descriptions of the importance of interior and exterior images for the creation of meaning and sense. Likely, too, they would assent to the value of visual memory for both recalling and understanding personal and sociocultural information, for they all engage, as Grandin pointed out, in using imagery in their thinking and expressive activities in one manner or another.

Peter, a nine-year-old boy with autism, demonstrated our "brain's representations of the world" and "thinking in pictures" at the same time he illustrated the iconic/narrative/image relationship in two small watercolor paintings he painted one warm morning as we sat together at my kitchen table, watching the sun chase shadows across the mountains that rimmed the far side of the valley. He was edgy from the moment he arrived at my door that day, distractedly scratching his arms and back as if he had hives, an indication of his disease. Nonetheless, despite his discomfort, Peter asked to paint, beginning as soon as he settled in the chrome and vinyl chair.

First he painted five swooping black scallops across the paper, the nearly opaque pigment forming a dense lowering band of cloudlike shapes (see Figure 3.1). Next, he placed an immense solid yellow disk below the curves, seemingly in the process of being blotted out, for the circle's top edge just grazed the sinking band, disappearing under the darker pigment. Peter set this painting aside and took another sheet of paper. Again he painted a heavy band of five or six black, scalloped cloudlike forms across the top. Next he added a circular brushstroke a third of the way down the paper, bracketing its hollow

Figure 3.1
Storm I, Peter, age eight, tempera on paper

shape with two jagged zigzags, their yellow seemingly repeating the hue of the circle. Below them, a thick undulating brushstroke of blue floated between two smaller shapes. The bottom of the paper was marked by a green ragged strip (see Figure 3.2). As a final gesture, he added his name in fading orange, between the blue and green forms. Wiggling now with misery and scratching vigorously, Peter put down his brush. He was through with art. Later that day I ran into his mother on the steep gravel path to their house. "How is he?" I inquired. "He is in his room," she sighed, clearly familiar with this turn of events. "He is feeling autistic."

I had encountered lowering clouds, bolts, and sun shapes before in Peter's art, for they appear frequently in his stress drawings, which seemingly herald the psychological state of Peter himself. As I watched, Peter had painted his storm conventions again, making clear his anxiety in solid visual forms as his obvious physiological discomfort grew. These symbols, these personal icons, all likely artistic primitives, all certainly familiar human forms—zigzag, circle, repeated hemispheres—cannot only be understood to be carriers of fierce meanings in Peter's art, of course. They also can be seen as the very shapes of Peter's mind, images simplified to their basic forms and part of his human inheritance. These images, though their message is a terrible one, are good to think; they are images presented with the simplicity of a single object, to be recognized as often as Peter or viewers encounter them.

Figure 3.2
Storm II, Peter, age eight, tempera on paper

The partial spheres, the spirals, and the circles return us to our earlier questions regarding the nature of such ubiquitous iconic forms and their relationship to more complex art images found in the visual world, for we have seen how human visual thinking skills create meaning through images and how our visual processes engage the world we inhabit to render the stuff of our lives comprehensible and concrete—a place to take action as well as pleasure in the material aspects of environment. We also have learned that though artists with and without autism share the same visual abilities, artists with autism, particularly children, allow a clearer view of shared human abilities, our "human birthright," the bright "shapes of our minds" in their less culturally obscured view of things. Additionally, we have seen these same bright shapes—outlines and linear constructs, human hands, faces, motions and postures, landscapes, the structural form of the visual world, particular patterns and shapes, the ability to use form, color, depth, and stereoscopic information independently of one another—describe many of the significant characteristics of images created by precocious young artists with autism, and other artists, too—vigorous, linear outlines and emphatic engagement with structure. We understand that the deep human pleasure found in creating and viewing aesthetic primitives that mirror both the artist's and the viewer's mind alike help to explain these young artists' delight, too. Most importantly, our new information offers an explanation for the appearance of precocious, vigorous, visually based drawing skills in very young, developmentally delayed artists. We have begun to see how our visual processes, a significant portion of our cognitive abilities, and the stuff of our memories are also a part of how we humans think, and that for some people, such as Grandin, visual imagery is a dominant aspect of cognition. Finally, we have glimpsed some of the cognitive processes by which we all, both those of us with and those without autism, construct our own personal narrative sense of meaning, our description of life in our world. Peter's scallops, swirls, and circles surely describe his being-in-the-world-at-that-moment just as clearly as Giacometti's figures indicate the sculptor's angst and despair, or the red zigzags describe a moment in the life of the young man in the red shorts that summer afternoon.

4

Jamie: Architect and Systems Planner

When Marilyn Zurmuehlen first introduced our graduate seminar to Nadia, the young girl with autism whose precocious drawings so amazed and perplexed Lorna Selfe (1977), we, too, were astonished both by the virtuosity of the drawings and by the young child who produced them. These images seemed to suggest many things—that art development was not only a bio-cultural process, that perceptually based drawings were produced not only in Western-style art classes, that drawing was perhaps linked to other physiological functions, and that the mystery that lies at the heart of human cognition and art making was deeper than any of us had previously imagined.

Years later, Jamie, an elementary-age boy with Asperger syndrome, a type of autism (Baron-Cohen, 1995; Frith, 1994, 1995; Happé, 1995), appeared in the class project of one of my education students. Like my student, I too, became fascinated with the precocious image making of this child. My investigation of young artists with autism, the types of images they create, and the possibility of narrative meaning found in the elements and compositional strategies of their art that had first been piqued in Marilyn's seminar years before, suddenly began to grow with my introduction to that young artist (Kellman, 1996, 1998). Zurmuehlen's previous explorations of the narrative aspect of art and the complexities of human creative behaviors as they relate to human physiology (Zurmuehlen, 1981, 1983, 1986, 1990, 1991), grounded my initial understanding of personal narrative and the stories of children with and without autism.

Now, several years after my first glimpse of Jamie's drawings and my own early investigations into the questions raised by precocious young artists with autism, it appears that within their frequently single-minded art, these young artists often tell their stories with a particular emphasis on three–dimensional drawing techniques and structural concerns as strategies for describing the world they have constructed or adopted as their own. This three–dimensional world also serves them as a foundation as they begin the difficult task of knitting their private inner world to the outer one of their family and society, using their art as a means both to reflect experience and convey meaning.

David Park (Park & Youderian, 1974), the father of Jessy, the creator of the superb view of the Duke University chapel, makes a similar point. He describes Jessy's elaborate system based on the relationship of numbers, light, colors, types of weather, phases of the moon, tableware, quantities of food, and ratings of time periods based on these attributes, writing, "It is clear if one talks to Jessy that many of the actions of people around her, and most of their intentions and concerns, have no meaning for her at all. It is our conjecture that the system of ideas described above represent Jessy's effort to fill the deficit by establishing her own kind of meaning" (p. 321). Now, as an adult, Jessy, who is enchanted by color, carries out similar examinations of hues, amounts, and architectural structures in brilliantly colored acrylic paintings, describing in images her own meaning and narrative based on quantities and complex visual relationships. Other people with autism, notably those with precocious artistic ability, also seem to create meaning through structure in their art. Structure, the "arrangement or interrelationship of all the parts of a whole" (*Webster's New Twentieth-Century Dictionary*, 1979), unlike composition, which refers to the combination of parts to form a unified whole, appears as a major component in the art of Stephen Wiltshire. Stephen (1987, 1989, 1991) provides a case in point, for as we have seen earlier, he draws architecture of all kinds—cities, individual buildings from skyscrapers to modest bungalows, and elaborate interiors—all in pen and ink or pencil. Stephen's eye is on the linear structure of his subjects, on their placement in space, and on the various elaborations of architectural detail. The description of architecture as shaping space provides an additional perspective on these drawings, for Stephen, who would like to be an architect, shapes space with each stroke of his pen. He employs foreshortening and perspective with an energetic, wiry line, constructing order through careful description of architecture that he sees, repeating the relationship of mass, form, direction, and weight.

The relationship of formal art elements to personal narrative is an important subject, for exploring it extends our understanding of these complex categories into a realm where usually only artists, teachers, and philosophers converse as they consider the most abstract nature of both art and meaning making. It is in turn from this more abstract inquiry that we will begin to develop our own understanding of how such apparently diverse elements as meaning and image interconnect to construct a narrative in terms of which "life makes sense" in the lives of both child and adult artists with and without autism. And we will come to realize that structure itself in both stories and art can also be seen to play an important role—as do forms themselves—as it acts as a descriptor and carrier of human emotions as part of the basic vocabulary of personal narrative itself.

Artist Ben Shahn (1985) clearly describes the artist's serious engagement with the complex relationships between structural issues, forms (which make up the structural elements, which, taken together, constitute composition), and meaning or content. He writes,

> It is the visible shape of man's growth; it is the living picture of his tribe at the most primitive, and of his civilization at its most sophisticated state. Form is the many faces of legend—bardic, epic, sculptural, musical, pictorial, architectural; it is the infinite images of religion; it is the expression and remnant of self. Form is the very shape of content. (p. 53)

This relationship of form (the elements that make up structure) and meaning making are found in children's art, too. In the art educator Marilyn Zurmuehlen's (1983) article on form and metaphor, she describes the narrative and pictorial devices used by young children, paying particular attention to repetition as an early structural device. She suggests that "repetition may be the most rudimentary aesthetic structure" and the meaning of children's pictures or stories is also "the mechanics," or "their form" (p. 117). She explains repetition as a means for elaborating an event or thing, or as a structure for occurrences, objects, or feelings primarily by the use of opposition or contrast. Mark making, according to Zurmuehlen (1983), partakes of similar uses of repetition. Examples include both repetitions of shapes and repetitions of contrast that "elaborate an event or object" (p. 115). Repetition as a structural device is also important when we take part in what Zurmuehlen (1990) calls the underlying condition of making art: "[a]s originators, transformers, and reclaimers, we participate in the sense of . . . once . . . now . . . then . . . that shapes our individual and collective life stories" (p. 65). This simple phrase " . . . once . . . now . . . then" can be understood to be the most basic form of narrative and of implied repetition, one that we all use to relate our life experiences. Our art making both announces our presence in the world and assures us of our existence in this simple structure that knits time and repetition together.

This use of repeated patterns is frequently found in the early stories and art of children as they engage one another in a mutual narrative enterprise using words, actions, and ideas, creating meaning in the mutual, repetitive text of play and dialogue. These repetitions—words, actions, and visual patterns—are not unlike the stories and plays created by Paley's (1990) preschool students in which the call and response of childen's voices weaves group activities into the fabric of a single playful narrative.

These early "almost stories," as Zurmuehlen (1983) calls them, demonstrate the use of repetitions as the basic structure, in the reiteration of words, concepts, and sounds, or in art's lines, shapes, and colors. Such stories provide their young creators with a useful means for creating dialogue and satisfying dramatic structure to share with other children or to act as metaphors and personal narratives in which the meaning lies in their mechanics or form. It is within the statement and restatement of various visual and auditory attributes that narrative presents itself; it is in the use of repetitions that meaning is both created and sustained. Young creators of spoken and drawn images confidently engage in making art as "originators, transformers, and reclaimers," as they live and describe their lives (Zurmuehlen, 1990, p. 65). The philosopher Susanne Langer (1953) helps us to understand this relationship of visual structure and meaning in art, since according to her, it is structure itself that allows for the presentation of the artist's feelings in forms that can be shared with others. At the same time, as feeling and imagination are expressed in these forms, intuition (an aspect of knowing through instantaneous comprehension) and meaning are created. In this way, structure, in addition to solidifying imagery visually, can be seen to contain within its lines, amounts, angles, and directionalities a relationship to meaning that is grounded in its physical characteristics (Langer, 1953). This returns us to our inquiry into structure and meaning in both art and narratives. Langer assures us not only of these intimate relationships but also that such forms clarify, organize, and create intuition, and through intuition, immediate understanding and meaning.

JAMIE

Our first young exemplar artist, Jamie, as yet unidentified as autistic but evidencing many of the characteristics of Asperger syndrome, demonstrates the specific use of form and structure to relate personal narrative meaning in his images. Repetitions of elements as aesthetic structures are also especially important to Jamie, a precocious seven-year-old artist in an academically gifted classroom, and his art.

Jamie's drawings, remarkable for a child his age, came to my attention as I graded the projects of my elementary education students exploring art making with children. The first drawing, a principal's suite complete with secretary's desk piled high with papers and a wall clock showing 1:55, reveals the principal's office through an open door on the left. A short el on the right leads to another door. Space and objects are meticulously drawn with single lines describing every surface, shifting with each change in angle or depth in the room or its contents. The principal, dressed in a shirt and slacks, eyes and glasses flying into the air with surprise and horror, confronts a teacher whose face and blouse drip a lumpy substance (mashed potatoes, I was to learn later). The teacher stands in misery, arms hanging at her sides, her outfit ruined. The details, foreshortening, perspective, and three-dimensional space are remarkable for a child of his age. Even the figures, though less sophisticated than the rendering of architectural space and objects, are what one might expect from a child of ten or eleven. I turn to the next two drawings. These images prove to be even more startling than the first. The second drawing (see Figure 4.1), an uninhabited living and dining room glimpsed through an open door, moves rapidly across the page from upper left to lower right. This panorama gives the sense that the artist stood in one place, turning his head from one side to another as he drew. The angle of vision tips slightly downward, as if the scene is observed leaning over a landing or bal-

Figure 4.1
Living Room, Jamie, age seven, ballpoint on paper

cony railing. Piano, carpets, and a variety of small objects are drawn in careful detail and in appropriate size relationship to one another. The subject of the drawing is not the contents but the room itself, its uninhabited space, and its wiring and electrical equipment. Wall sockets, complete with plug receptors, as well as wall switches appear at regular intervals around the room. The video player, surrounded by tapes in the center of the floor, is attached to the television in the lower left. Floor and wall lamps send out light rays. Switch chains wiggle. Wires from the boom box, head phones, lamp, and extension cord twist and turn. The drawing is alive with energy.

Drawing number three, another uninhabited interior moving from left to right, exhibits a style I come later to recognize as Jamie's. It, too, is energized by sockets and lamps. At the top of the paper floats a diagram of an exterior deck. The reverse side of the drawing includes a second-floor hall, in the familiar left-to-right downward angle. Attic space and a small section of roof laid out in planes floats above the hall. These drawings appear to me to be similar to Stephen's skillful use of energetic pen and pencil outlines to investigate architecture, and Nadia's vigorous line drawings of horses (Selfe, 1977).

Several months later I was able to follow the thread of Jamie's art further by interviewing his second-grade teacher. According to him, Jamie has outstanding language skills, writes imaginative stories about nearly everything, and, like Stephen, wants to be an architect. He emphasized that Jamie talks a great deal when asked a question, as if there is no one else in the room. While talking, he is turned around in his seat, looking at the wall. The teacher considers him a creative child, a good little artist who draws all the time. He works well with others if asked to do so but otherwise prefers to be solitary. He has his way of doing things and is somewhat inflexible. For example, he has never used the school bathroom, though his teacher has recently persuaded him to wash his hands at noon.

I also met with Jamie and his mother, a kindergarten teacher, during one warm Southern summer. On my first visit, Jamie, a small, delicate child with brown eyes and tousled brown hair, wearing a striped T-shirt and green shorts and clutching his black kitten, Kit-Kat, was right behind his mother, talking, as the door opened. He immediately informed me that he wanted to be an architect. "I'm drawing the Promenade Room now . . . I was so excited when I saw *The Towering Inferno* for sale at the grocery last night," he continued, as if this explained everything. He led me to the corner of the living room where a small drafting table stood in the glow of the screw-on lamp. Immediately, Jamie began to display everything in his portfolio, describing, without stopping to take a breath, each drawing in detail. He explained where each drawing was done, the date it was finished, the source of its content, as well as the drawing problems he encountered—his struggle to portray a spiral staircase (see Figure 4.2),

Figure 4.2
Stairway, *The Towering Inferno*, Jamie, age seven, pencil on paper

for example, or the complexities of drawing the Promenade Room at the top of a skyscraper after a fistfight and riot had taken place. Most drawings centered on architecture and its details, though automobiles are important. Many focused on systems and categories—wiring, a page of clocks, computers, control rooms, dashboards, engines. All were done in ballpoint pen or pencil. Only a few contained color; if color was used, it appeared arbitrary and careless, applied as an afterthought when the drawing was complete. Few drawings contained people or other living creatures. Catastrophe or disarray reigned in most images—fires, car crashes, riots, and the ravages of decay and neglect appeared regularly. Almost all his drawings included foreshortening and other perspectival descriptions of an object in space (see Figure 4.3).

Jamie talked ceaselessly about his drawings, apparently uninterested in a response. His mother, used to this state of affairs, talked over him, hushing him so that she, too, could make a remark. She described Jamie's art, which began suddenly when he was five with a drawing of a table and chair and an image of the inside of a church. In this drawing there is a figure, a minister in the pulpit (Jamie's grandfather is a minister), an unusual presence in Jamie's world of an-

Figure 4.3
Traffic Jam, Jamie, age seven, pencil on paper

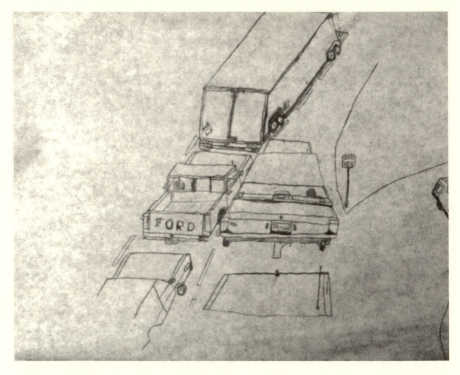

gles and wiring. Jamie's next drawings were of the rooms in Mr. Hall's house, an imaginary dwelling for an imaginary man. From these early interiors he moved to drawing the exteriors of houses, all with numerous basement ventilators. His mother explained that Jamie had been especially fascinated by these grillwork openings but that his current interests were elevators and cars, especially their dashboards and engines. Just like his first drawing, Jamie's ideas just seem to appear, according to his mother.

Jamie nibbled delicately at his hands in between pointing out details in his drawings or clasped them tightly between his knees as he wiggled with excitement. Later, when I patted his shoulder in thanks for a job well done, he winced, dropping down and sideways to avoid my hand. It was as if I had burned him. Finished with his art for a time, Jamie left the room, returning moments later eating chocolate, his favorite food.

He threw himself on the couch without a glance at either his mother or me. His demeanor announced that he was through with us. He was off to something else. He did not say goodbye as I left, even though his mother asked him to do so, nor did he stop eating his candy, even though his mother requested it.

My next visit followed the same pattern—Jamie talking constantly, obsessively describing details and actions in his several new drawings, including a burning skyscraper (*The Towering Inferno*, he assured me); The Promenade Room before and after a drunken fight (see Figure 4.4); and several three-quarter views of Delorean cars and engines in exquisite detail (see Figure 4.5). After an hour spent looking at Jamie's new creations, we moved to his playroom, a small space with a computer and wall-to-wall Legos—Lego accessories, figures, vehicles—to see Jamie's constructions, cars, and environments. The moment he was seated in the midst of the bright plastic windows, bricks, and roof sections, Jamie began a multistory structure with an external staircase and two glass brick walls. His mother and I talked quietly about their family and about Jamie, who was absorbed in his building. Jamie has trouble sleeping even though he works on his drawings and Legos for five or more hours at a stretch, she told me, and she takes him to the swimming pool every afternoon to tire him out. Suddenly, Jamie joined the conversation, describing his pleasure in eating the puckered skin from his hands at the swimming pool, chewing down to the "clean new skin underneath." He then returned quietly to his building project, working without another word until I left.

Figure 4.4
Promenade Room, Jamie, age seven, pencil on paper

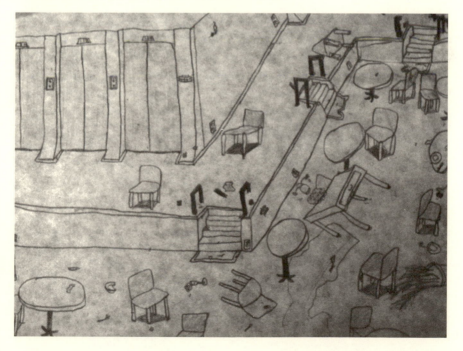

Figure 4.5
Delorean Dashboard, Jamie, age seven, pencil on paper

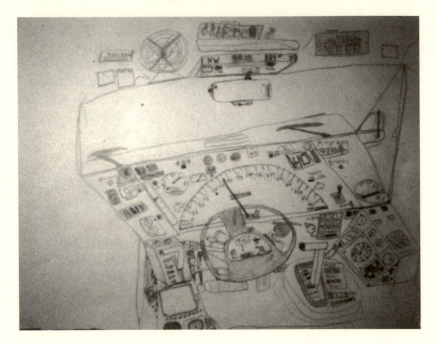

Visits with Jamie follow a pattern—Jamie talking constantly about *The Towering Inferno* and other action pictures, Jamie describing details from the latest installment of his favorite television program *The Price Is Right* (he is especially fond of the lights and special effects), or Jamie explaining his new drawings. Out of this hodgepodge of images, conversations, and repeated subject matter, this young architect and systems planner organizes his time and experiences through the medium of his drawings, explaining to himself and to everyone who sees them the relationship of his personal narrative to drawing structure and the space it contains. Jamie's memories of when and where each drawing was completed helps him organize his understanding of where he has been, what he has done, and where he might go next. They create and illustrate his personal history in the manner of a time line through such concrete images as the beach house where his family stayed last summer, the messy versus clean teenager's room drawings he created during the Super Bowl, a drawing he completed last week when his family ate in a restaurant, and so on.

Jamie's interest in systems, architecture, wiring, gauges and dials, and chaos as well as his precocity all may reflect autism. Though, like other artists with autism, Jamie's work may have its roots in "autistic obsessions" and perseverations, "it allows her [or him] to make something beautiful out of what otherwise would be dismissed" (Park, 1994, p. 250) as well as to create and express his own meanings and stories. This probable grounding in autism does not explain his art away, however. As Oliver Sacks (1995) points out, remarking on Stephen Wiltshire's perceptual clarity and unconceptualized view of the world, it is the perceptual "thisness" of Stephen's vision that draws us in, "the catching of 'thisness,'" of "perceptual genius" (p. 242). The same may be said of Jamie's idiosyncratic drawings, too, and the story they tell of the "thisness" of his daily life. If one considers what Jamie's drawings are doing with "thisness," what their underlying subject really is, it becomes clear that, like Stephen, he shapes space while drawing architecture structure, repeatedly creating forms that encompass both real and imagined events in his life (Kellman, 1996). The energetic nature of Jamie's drawings, the "thisness" of the places that he inhabits or imagines, pulls the observer into Jamie's world and into the excitement of place and space rendered alive and trembling with energy. Philosopher Gaston Bachelard (1994) writes of the insistent quality of drawings of such inhabited, created space. He points out that a well-executed likeness "leads to contemplation and dreaming. Daydreams return to inhabit an exact drawing" (p. 49). Jamie, too, has the ability to render place and space in this vivid manner, as he outlines each recession and raised surface of an edifice or vehicle with a sure hand and rich detail.

Jamie's tightly structured perspectival drawings are fine examples of Bachelard's notion that "space contains compressed time. That is what space is for" and may serve as calendars for his life in their amalgam of past events and future plans (Bachelard, 1994, p. 8). Jamie's linear, perspectival, foreshortened images describe in their repeated forms and emphatic construction his own story as they pull his history—school activities, family experiences, fictional stories, special interests, and daily life—into a visible, narrative whole that includes a future, too, one that itself grows from the fertile soil of structure and forms (Kellman, 1996, 1998). This elaborate use of structure, repeated in daily drawings, provides Jamie a web of meaning that is firmly based on his repeated visual forms and subjects in a manner not too dissimilar from Jessy's complex system of light and numbers, or, in another fashion, other autistic children's habitual actions of blowing on soup or lining up toys. As Park and Youderian (1974) point out in regard to Jessy, construction of meaning appears to underlie her system building; it is likely that for Jamie his drawings are just such systems made visible. Bachelard (1994) enlarges our perspective of this relationship of memory and form when he writes, "Memories are motionless, and the more securely they are fixed in space, the sounder they are" (p. 9). Surely Jamie documents and solidifies his world through these drawings in a similar manner, describing what he sees, imagines, and enjoys, presenting the story of his world in the solid lines of his drawings.

Complex as the creative act is for a nonautistic artist, artists with autism face an additional challenge. Turned in on themselves by autism and denied meaning in the social world, the visible becomes for them a most significant, concrete presence, one that they may knit into the flux of personal lived experience to create a meaningful whole. Not unlike nonautistic artists who also struggle with creating meaning and structure grounded in the visible, artists with autism attempt to produce an edifice that includes a sense of their own agency as well as a past, present, and future, however isolated from the rest of the sociocultural world.

Art's role in both individual and collective life lies beyond its immediately discerned surface attributes, decorative possibilities, and current social functions. For art in its very substance and structure provides individual artists—Jamie and others—with a sense of mastery, meaning, and coherence at the same time that it affords viewers a glimpse of artistic resolve and personal narrative. It is in this manner that art and its many narratives binds us together with a language we all share as we confront our common human struggles, our individual disasters, and our personal triumphs, for as Barry Lopez (1981) reminds us, "That is all that is holding us together" (p. 62), our stories and our empathetic understanding of the truth of one another's lives.

Drawing with Peter:
Narrative and Art

DRAWING AND TALKING

High-functioning autism was diagnosed in Peter Anderson after he failed to acquire language by the age of three. Susan, his mother, began to draw pictures with him, hoping these images might provide a link between the life of their family and the chaotic, tantrum-wracked world of her son, in a manner that language had not been able to do. Using a pencil on ordinary, lined notebook paper, Susan repeatedly drew the floor plan of their house, the location and shape of the objects in it, and characters in movies that Peter enjoyed, especially his favorite, *The Wizard of Oz*. Susan's plans, maps, images, and her words that accompanied them were an attempt to not only introduce Peter to language, but also to entice him to take part in the world around him. Susan's use of language and drawing did not lead to immediate success, however. One day Peter lost his teddy bear somewhere in the house. Susan, who knew the bear lay on the kitchen table, drew a rough plan of their dwelling, talking about each room and its pieces of furniture, stressing locations and relationships among the various parts and objects. Finally, she drew the table, enumerating its characteristics and indicating its location. "He found the table all right," she ruefully remarked, "but he never did find that big, old bear" (Kellman, 1999a).

This incident from Peter's early life goes directly to the heart of the matter, for it describes his introduction to image as map, as communication, and as a means to engage the world itself, even before he himself could pick up a pencil. It was in this manner that drawing as both tool and as alternative world first took root in Peter's life and developed over time into his most complex expressive language as well as his most absorbing activity.

Now, at the age of eight, Peter's drawings are astonishing in both their quantity and variety as evidenced by the hundreds of drawings collected by his mother since the beginning of his art making. These include (1) intense, jagged pen or pencil sketches of Peter's interior turmoil that form the bulk of his output; (2) carefully worked, schematic images of favorite stories that imply three–dimensionality created in colored marker or pencil; (3) line drawings often emphasizing motion, foreshortening, and other three-dimensional qualities of characters from books or movies; and (4) fanciful, two–dimensional depictions in colored or graphite pencil of his favorite authors or domestic scenes grounded in reality. This wide variety of drawing styles, line qualities, spatial considerations, and topics evokes an almost irresistible desire to inquire into the origins and meanings of such diversity in the work of a single young artist with autism. At the same time, each type of drawing seems to be firmly linked to a particular style. What might such linkage tell us? What might explain the different stylistic categories? How does art seem to function for Peter? What do Peter's drawings suggest about art itself? And how, like other artists, might this young artist with autism also experience himself in art making in the now familiar narrative form of ". . . once . . . now . . . then . . . that shapes our individual and collective life stories"?

FAVORITE STORIES, ART AS COMMUNICATION

Susan's more narrative drawings, especially those of Oz, were occasions for storytelling in Peter's early years, allowing both Susan and Peter to follow a well-known tale through all its familiar developments. Oz and its characters were specially explored, as Peter watched his Oz video by the hour, absorbed in the adventures of Dorothy and her friends. As Peter's fascination with Oz continued over time, his room became a kind of Oz, with every available space crammed with bright statuettes of its characters, colorful posters, action toys and dolls, anything that contained an image from Oz. These images appear to have solidified a pattern for art making that Peter follows even today as he enters third grade (see Figure 5.1). Not only is the Oz story in its many manifestations still one of his major preoccupations, but drawing its characters and discussing the story or L. Frank Baum, the author, are nearly daily activities. During second grade, at Peter's insistence, he and his classmates even pro-

Figure 5.1
Characters from *The Wizard of Oz*, Peter, age seven, ballpoint on paper

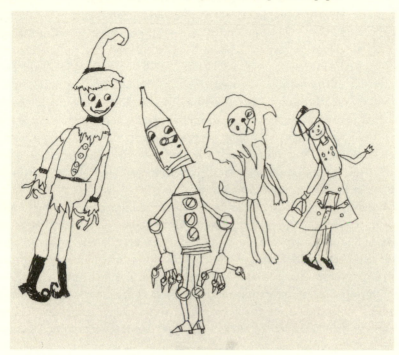

duced *The Wizard of Oz* as a play, complete with realistic costumes, stage make-up, and simple scenery.

With exposure to other stories at home and at school, Peter's literary interests have begun to expand. Now *The Lord of the Rings,* fairy tales including *Rapunzel, The Snow Queen, The Three Little Pigs, James and the Giant Peach, Peter Pan, Alice in Wonderland, The Magic School Bus,* and several action and horror movies appear as subject matter in both his art and his conversation. Such stories often are the occasion for drawing performance posters—posters advertising a movie or play of *James and the Giant Peach* , for example, or *Peter Pan.* The posters are done in colored marker with heavy black outlines. The figures, in threes and fours, move across the paper in a steep diagonal, which implies deep space, at the same time they lead the viewer's eye from bottom left to top right, or they march across a firm baseline at the bottom of the paper. Unlike many Western, nonautistic children his age (Alland, 1983; Davis, 1998; Gardner & Winner, 1982; Lowenfeld & Brittain, 1987; Strauss, 1982), other three–dimensional characteristics creep into Peter's art in a manner reminiscent of several other precocious young artists with autism. This early and frequently precocious use of visually based three–dimensional drawing skills has been recognized as a particular attribute of the art of young artists with autism, as has the beginning of such skills when a child is three or four years of age (Grandin, 1995b; Kellman, 1996, 1998; Park, 1994; Selfe, 1977; Wiltshire, 1987, 1989, 1991). Though not as three–dimensionally grounded as the art of such notable young artists as Jamie, Steven Wiltshire, or Nadia when she was young (Kellman, 1996, 1998; Selfe, 1977; Wiltshire, 1984, 1989, 1991), Peter is still able to use three–dimensional drawing skills in some of his drawings. Tables frequently display foreshortening, for example, and animate figures are solid, dimensional, and vigorous, often displaying a closely observed turn in legs, body, or head. Overlapping is also frequent. Text is often present, too, with thick black letters that read "*The Wizard of Oz* a comedy, based on the book by L. Frank Baum, play by Peter Anderson," or "Lewis Caroll's [sic] Alices [sic] *Adventures in Wonderland.*"

A second group of Oz drawings, far outnumbering Peter's colored images, are figures, done with pencil or pen on lined paper. These active, lively images include Baum's Patchwork Girl and Oz characters and, less frequently, characters from Peter's other favorite stories. The figures are lifelike, exhibiting foreshortening, three–dimensionality, spatial rotation, and a vigor that belies their origins in the realm of cartoon and make-believe. Some of these drawings apparently fail at the outset, for Peter draws only a single hand, head, or leg and tosses them aside. First seen fully formed by Peter in a well-defined, easily controlled environment and in a variety of formats, his favorite characters provide him subjects for drawings that, in their turn, provide him with a pleasing level of stimulation that can be repeatedly explored at will.

Perhaps these undemanding narratives, controlled and created by Peter in a variety of media, free him from the need to respond except as he chooses, at the same time granting him permission to absorb every detail of their visual qualities and familiar narratives. Peter readily shows the completed fantasy/video drawings and poster images to others, inquiring if the viewer has read the book, or seen the movie or video. "Do you know L. Frank Baum?" "Do you know Cinderella?" "Do you know Roald Dahl?" he asks. No matter what the answer, these literary/video drawings provide Peter with worlds that are limited, proscribed, and familiar, worlds that he can both inhabit and share with others, especially peers, with whom sociability is most difficult.

THE ACTUAL WORLD, ART AS DESCRIPTION

Authors themselves have become subjects for Peter to draw and discuss, as have the illustrators of several classic tales. As Peter draws his own version of *Alice,* his conversation is a mixture of references to the original narrative, the illustrations, the author, and the illustrator, seemingly mingled in a single, mutual reality. At the same time, these drawings are semi-mythic in nature, pulling together elements of the author's own creations with aspects of their actual lives, turning both the writers and artists into characters in their own creations. Usually drawn with a fine-pointed graphite or colored pencil or a ballpoint pen, these drawings bridge the world of narrative fantasy and actual biographic experience.

In his detailed pencil drawing of J.R.R. Tolkien, for example, Peter shows the author as an elfish figure seated in an ornate high-backed chair next to a ta-

Figure 5.2
J.R.R. Tolkien, Peter, age eight, pencil on paper

ble piled with copies of his books (see Figure 5.2). Smoke from his pipe rises into the air in rings, coalescing into the forms of a Hobbit and of Smaug, the dragon, who flies, breathing flames overhead, as Peter is happy to point out. In another case, Peter's drawing of Thomas Wolfe's boyhood home, depicted as a haunted house with crumbling facade fancifully situated next to a cemetery complete with angel grave marker, memorializes the local celebrity in ballpoint pen. This drawing, less detailed and sophisticated than the drawing of Tolkien, nonetheless catches some of the dreary feel of Wolfe's boyhood home as well as the elegiac quality of his first novel, *Look Homeward Angel*.

These author/artist images, unlike Peter's poster art, are in the current Walt Disney studio style, a simplified Victorian aesthetic that leans heavily on curved lines, ornate decorative elements, and elfish, flattened characters that nonetheless still exploit foreshortening and motion with a single wiry line. Even the Disney conventions of mice in the baseboard and spy holes in the eyes of pictures are present in these drawings. This cartooned quality is not surprising, however, for Disney movies and videos form a major portion of Peter's free-time fare, and the Disney studio itself figures as a character in his imaginary world of movies, narratives, future plans, and drawing preoccupations.

Another category of drawings based on the real world are those grounded in Peter's actual lived experience. One particular example is notable: a drawing of the Andersons themselves, their house, and their pets.

"Oo—oo boy, this is hard," Peter remarks to himself after a few minutes of struggling with his drawing of his family home, for the first time at a loss for what to draw. The curve of the Andersons' hill rising in the center of the page presents no difficulty, nor do the tight, jagged lines indicating the gravel driveway. However, the house itself, perched on the top of the rise, gives Peter considerable pause. After several false starts, he finally produces a house, a tropical island–like structure of roof, legs, and central platform (see Figure 5.3). The dwelling's scanty elements include five red posts rising vertically from the hill; a large, flat, red deck; a central blue rectangular door; a short, slanted red rail that angles upward from the deck to a small brown square ("our jacuzzi," Peter remarks); and a red triangle on two posts ("a roof so things will not get wet"). Near the door and on one side of the main deck, an almost invisible white structure hovers under a green and orange scalloped form. If one tilts the paper, a post with tripod legs, a central horizontal surface, and an L-shaped form appear, revealing themselves as the umbrella-shaded table where Peter's family often eats during the warm months.

Above the jacuzzi, Heidi the cat sticks her tongue out at Bear the puppy (whom Peter does not like), as they face off from opposite sides of the roof. The Andersons themselves stand on the hill to the left of the house, their size, clothing, and hair length indicating their identity. To the right of the dwelling

Figure 5.3
The Andersons' House, Peter, age eight, colored pencil on paper

lies a flower bed and fountain, a mermaid in its center raising her arms in a gesture similar to Peter's mother and sister on the opposite side of the hill. Behind
the rock-edged flower border in front and to one side of the fountain, a green,
semi-circular hill rises steeply, setting off the red blooms below and forming a
base for the three trees and leafless vine that lean, as if in a gale, toward the
house. Drawn in a Western, socioculturally grounded, schematic manner using a ground line and both form and color schema (Alland, 1983; Davis, 1998;
Gardner & Winner, 1982; Lowenfeld & Brittain, 1987; Pariser & van den

Berg, 1997; Strauss, 1982), the house image contains none of the elaborate curlicues and stereotyped details of Peter's Hollywood/children's literature images. His active, three-dimensional style, so evident in his Oz drawings, is not in evidence either. Perhaps because I had suggested this reality-based subject matter, or because Peter is afraid to be outside and could not, therefore, fully attend to the appearance of the house and its surroundings, or because his ability to distinguish figure/ground relationships is poor, or because of autism's egocentric focus, or for another reason altogether, the human figures are hastily sketched creations with simple red and blue clothing, and the trees are simplified versions of Peter's usual emphatic leaning tree schema. It is the house itself that stands out as the clear subject of the image, both for its unusual characteristics and for its central placement in Peter's picture.

One of the differences between this drawing and Peter's other art is that the image is based on his life experience, rather than a film, illustration, or commercially produced image. There are no previous models for Peter to reproduce, and most importantly, no physical and psychic distance between Peter and his subject matter as there is in his renditions of commercially produced images. These differences, however, do not seem to explain the diverse collection of structural elements that make up Peter's house, nor the fact that the house is barely physically present, even though it is at the vital center of the drawing.

The structural elements depicted in Peter's drawing are aspects of the house that he himself frequently touches or uses. For example, the porch supports, front door, and deck railings, all elements that Peter encounters daily as he enters and leaves his home, form a major portion of his image. The floor of the main deck that serves as entry walkway, outside dining room, and play surface, as well as the jacuzzi a short stairway above that Peter frequently shares with his family, are shown as solid structures, as is the table where the family eats almost every day in good weather. These exterior elements of the Andersons' home, encountered by Peter physically and repeatedly in a variety of ways, at various times of the day and year, make up his image of his family's house, with the addition of a peaked roof instead of the flat one of the actual dwelling. The remainder of the house is of little consequence, it seems. Walls are perhaps more interior than exterior experiences—a place for windows, posters, curtains, and shelves, enclosing space, but not necessary in the outside world. In a similar manner, the chimney, which does not have an active role in Peter's life, and the windows, which likely serve as openings from the inside out (more holes to look through than physical entities), do not appear.

Pets and family, posed outside the house, are also an important physical part of Peter's life, demanding, soothing, feeding, playing with, and caring for him by turns. Drawn as schema, stiff, simplified, and motionless, both family and pets nonetheless play a part in Peter's understanding of both home and house. Only the fountain and flowers, though they exist in fact, are drawn in anything like his familiar vocabulary of Disney schema, where mermaids inhabit fountains in castle courtyards and fairies swoop through bright-colored flower gardens.

This personal drawing, grounded in Peter's daily experience, is as interesting for what is included as for what is not. The physical world of the Andersons' domestic exterior space is reduced to the objects used by, or of interest to, Peter himself. Nothing else appears. Even his family, unlike his favorite authors, directors, or movie stars, are reduced to simple schema, unindividualized and inanimate, rather like the age-appropriate, two-dimensional schema of humans to be found in Jamie's art (Kellman, 1996). Peter's house/family drawing is a visual list of architectural elements and family members, in which his egocentric reductionist view of the world is the basis for the selection of image elements and compositional choices. However, this curious drawing serves Peter as a map, as well as a list, for it allows him the opportunity to locate himself within his family constellation and home environment and provides a means of envisioning himself in the midst of his own actual experience.

CHAOS DRAWINGS, ART AS EXPRESSION OF EMOTION

By far the largest number of drawings in the five cartons and piles of loose paper Mrs. Anderson delivered to me at my arrival were what she and other family members refer to as "Peter's stress reliever art." These hasty drawings, done while Peter was feeling agitated—"feeling autistic," according to his mother—illustrate his state of mind from deep within his psyche. For Peter, like many autistic children, "[t]emper tantrums, aggressiveness, destructiveness, without any apparent awareness of the effects on others are common, especially in response to interference with repetitive activities or changes in the environment." And as with some children, this behavior seems to be associated with "high levels of anxiety" (Wing, 1994, p. 95). The scrawled drawings are in many ways similar to Peter's other art, for they have their own set of repetitions and conventions that he revisits repeatedly both at home and during school in his own time-out drawing carrel. Wild jagged lines laced with lightning bolts, electric sparks shooting in all directions, dark boiling clouds and tornado cones, violent scribbles, a huge monster who orchestrates chaos, and a sunken-eyed, scrawny character with clawlike, black hands, manacled at the neck to the turbulent center of the storm, are repeated in varying combinations in nearly every stress drawing (see Figure 5.4). Often completed in a matter of seconds, these drawings appear to enable Peter to discharge his anxieties and regain control of himself both at home and at school.

Figure 5.4
Stress Drawing, Peter, age unknown, ballpoint on paper

   One drawing in this category is of special interest, for it pulls together both the world of Oz and the frightening disintegration of Peter's stress release drawings. In the foreground, almost unrecognizable because of their small scale, the figure of a little girl with braids and a tiny black dog run across the yard of a miniature farmhouse and barn. Above the thin strands of sky that barely shelter their heads, the familiar powerful storm witch with empty smile hovers, lightning sizzling from tonglike fingers, as black clouds sweep across the top of the paper. This particular drawing perhaps best illustrates Peter's situation, for the unbearable sense of unseen danger and impending disaster that seems to hover over Dorothy and Toto likely illustrates Peter's own fearful and oblique approach to the world around him. The underlying narrative becomes clear in a manner not glimpsed in the other drawings of chaos and disintegration, for the true menace of psychic unmaking can be felt in the minuscule fleeing figures, helpless and terrified before the enormity of the all-powerful and invincible witch. In this drawing, it seems, even the golden world of Oz can be threatened by the chaos of uncontrollable violence that lurks just at the edge of its reality, ready to appear without warning, shattering Oz's careful structure with the suddenness of a thunderstorm.

DRAWINGS OF THE FUTURE, ART AS IMAGINING

Another of Peter's drawings, a bright Disney-like fantasy of stereotyped cats, mice, magic motifs, and baroque furniture, also appears to bridge two worlds. This colorful drawing layers cartoon fantasies onto Peter's current plans for the future, to run a bookstore with his mother that is as full of cats as it is of books, similar to the one with which he is familiar in a nearby town.

In the center of the drawing, a purple chair of curved lines and tendril-like forms perches uneasily on two legs next to a red, two-legged table; the furniture, the focal point of the image, clings to the wildly slanting baseline, which bisects the page. A red and yellow fringed rug hangs an inch below the table and chair, as if on a wash line. Four identical red cats with perked ears and clubby tails raised to their right in slight curves sit at intervals under, on, and next to the table. Open books and mice accompany each cat. A blue cloud with stars and a slender black, purple, and red rainbow rises from one book. A blue mouse springs from the pages of another. A red thunderhead, topped with a magnifying glass, an eye peering through its center, hovers over yet another. A gray mouse with magnifying glass and a mouse hole lies beyond one cat's tail. A candelabra, spider, and web hang from the center of a ceiling line in the center of the room. Evenly spaced purple squares rise above the ceiling, five with small skulls inside. Inside the other, "Peter Anderson" is printed carefully. The placement of the table and chair is similar to Peter's Tolkien drawing and the conventions of a central table, spiders and webs, skulls, and magic all can be found in several of his other drawings, too. In this superimposition of future and Disney-like fantasy, Peter knits together what he knows, what he enjoys, and what he imagines into a single image. His fascination with the conventions of the forces of magic, his interest in books and narrative, and his overwhelming absorption in the world of Disney are all projected forward into the future. "When I am twelve, I'm going to open a bookstore with my mom. A cat bookstore," he announces with assurance. Peter's art allows him to envision a future that provides both continuity with the life he lives and concrete representations of how such a future might appear. It allows him to create a solid, satisfying center, a place to locate himself in a world that for him is often chaotic and difficult.

Peter's various kinds of art provide him a world he controls, a means of communication, a socially acceptable method for dealing with stress and anxiety, a future as well as a present. Using various understandings of the visible world he has found in movies, videos, books, illustrations, and his own life, Peter engages in creating art from the content of both his inner and outer worlds. His art gives him the power to explore both at once, an example of the creative process, engaged in an integrative activity of the most important kind in which he is able, like Jamie (and everyone else for that matter), to find the story that explains the events of his life at least to himself, to find the narrative that gives his life both meaning and sense.

One of the most easily seen features of Peter's drawings are the four separate categories of compositional style and their distinctive contents. Each has its own visual vocabulary, line quality, space, type of form, and approach to detail and color. Each takes place under separate circumstances in Peter's life, and each features different drawing strategies and styles, creating a language of visual forms to tell his story. These four categories taken together suggest that Peter's art images differ, depending upon the content and emotional function of each drawing; his art is unlike the socioculturally grounded schema that one might expect from a child of his age in this culture and society. Peter's art seems to imply that image development may be driven, in his case at least, more by the psychic proximity of subject matter and its narrative and autobiographical function than by other concerns. In other words, types of images may have to do more with making meaning or personal narrative for Peter rather than other considerations or sociocultural causes (Kellman, 1999a). This, as we have discovered, has significance for all young artists, with or without autism. Young children, like everyone else, struggle to create meaning and sense from their experiences and the events of their lives. Art can be viewed as an important means for a child to construct an inner world that provides personal meaning through the graphic interpretation of his or her world, rather than merely being a way for a child to idle away time or as part of a therapeutic plan. At the same time, art also enables a child to examine his or her connections with others while simultaneously providing each viewer an opportunity to engage in his or her own acts of interpretation. As Peter's describing, telling, and drawing interweaves personal events with well-known stories and other images has shown, his art, like Jamie's, not only informs us of his own story and struggle to construct a meaningful, manageable world, but also suggests the importance of what we might call the language of forms, a visual language that uses elements of visual structure to create and relate the artist's narrative.

THE BOYS, A FURTHER COMPARISON

As we have come to see, Peter can be said to construct his world and a sense of coherence from an amalgamation of Disney studio productions and Hollywood film conventions—sources that supply him with styles, conventions, and stories that allow him to devise a body of images "in terms of which his life makes sense" (Zurmuehlen, 1987). Including such diverse elements as *The Wizard of Oz*, a local bookstore, and *Alice in Wonderland*, Peter utilizes his art to create meaning and a sense of order in his experience. At the same time, he describes a psychic place that contains a past, present, and future—a linear foundation for the formulation of a solid self. Peter's several styles spring from this narrative, meaning-making intention, for in his three–dimensional images, scribbles, and combinations of styles, he frames his personal story in the language of line and form that can be read by both the artist and his audience. His art also provides him an acceptable social role as class artist, serving as a useful subject for social interaction and an "invitation to interpretation" for both peers and adults (Zurmuehlen, 1987).

Jamie, too, grounds himself within his visual narratives, for like Peter, he creates a psychic location that includes a future as it describes his present embedded in images of local architecture, favorite stories, and movies. Just as Jamie's narratives provide temporal orientation, so, too, they provide an ordered world, allowing him to originate meaning from the satisfyingly controllable aspects of his favorite buildings and adventures. Jamie, it seems, uses his structurally based images' visual order to provide a template for the formulation of a sense of self in the repeatable relationships of architecture, auto design, and systems layouts. These subjects illustrate integrated experiences in terms of which Jamie's own narrative becomes understandable. Just as his art gives meaning and unity to his experiences through narrative, it also serves to engage others in their own acts of comprehension. It is in this manner that integration of Jamie's social sphere and his personal narrative comes about, for other people are drawn into his world by the vigor and expertise of his drawings (Kellman, 1999b). As Zurmuehlen might point out, Jamie's art frames a narrative that provides a means of constructing a self out of the welter of his unfiltered experiences. She writes, "Authentic art transforms our experiences of context so that we reclaim the personal and particular from a mire of everydayness" (1986, p. 36). It is through that "personal and particular" experience of what was previously undistinguished sensation that Jamie's art likely gives meaning to his experience, and it transforms the "everydayness" of his undifferentiated exterior and interior space into a text he can share with others.

As we have seen, repetition in children's art and narrative also plays an important role in developing structure. It is not unlikely that for Peter as well as Jamie the repetition of images, motifs, drawing strategies, and stories also play a similar formative role; and though perhaps the repetitive nature of the boys' imagery can be understood to relate to autistic perseveration and interests, it is also possible to imagine such repetition as an attempt to create narrative form. None of this meaning making, narrative, and particularity in the boys' art should surprise us, however, for as we have seen, "the essential conditions for making art include artistic causality, idiosyncratic meaning, and intentional symbolization" (Zurmeuhlen, 1990, p. 63). And most certainly we can see the "essential conditions of making art" in the creations of Jamie, Peter, and other children, too, as well as their certain participation in the construction of narrative meaning in the varied forms of their richly illustrated stories.

6

Making Real: Katie and Mark

In *The Velveteen Rabbit*, first published in 1922 by Margery Williams (1991), little Rabbit, a stuffed animal, inquires of the Skin Horse, another, older toy, "'What is REAL? . . . Does it mean having things that buzz inside you and a stick-out handle?'" The Skin Horse replies, "'REAL isn't how you are made. . . . It's something that happens to you.'" The Skin Horse continues, answering little Rabbit's questions concerning the nature of being and the process of creating such a condition through experience and relationships. "'It doesn't happen all at once,' said the Skin Horse. 'You become. It takes a long time.'" He explains further, "'Once you become REAL, you can't become unreal again. It lasts for always'" (p. 5). This conversation between the Skin Horse and Rabbit takes place as the younger toy considers for the first time the property of relationships between creatures in a shared world and the nature of being and reality. The rabbit's desire to become real, to engage the world in a new and more meaningful manner, to engage in relationship, is similar to the impulse that drives the artist to make manifest, to make "real" the many narratives that both form and originate from her life. Similarly, it is a longing to remember, order, make sense of, and express the flow of time and experience that children, too, address as they tell stories and make images that, by their nature, bind them to others and to the world. They, like little Rabbit, demonstrate the desire to become "real" in the myriad forms of their elaborate, imagined constructions.

Four girls in two cultures serve as our introduction to yet another young girl, a child experiencing autism, who likewise describes her domestic world of steaming meals and social interactions with similar attention to the richness of visual imagery and the vividness of experience. We will begin with a simple supper in the highlands of Guatemala, move to a tea party in Iowa, and then meet Katie over a hot dinner in a world populated with vigorous animals as well as Katie and her family.

The two five-year-old Maya girls, dressed in long skirts and colorful *huipiles*, or blouses, their black hair untidy after a long day of play, sat on their knees on a small square of blue plastic, talking quietly to each other as they worked. The girl closest to the covered porch, Rosa, patted dark green heart-shaped impatiens leaves like tortillas between her hands, alternating positions with each pat as she has seen her mother do every day of her short life. When the tiny "tortillas" had achieved their proper thickness (determined apparently by the number of pats and actions, not the leaf itself), the girl placed it in the neatly spaced rows of other leaves in front of her on the blue sheet. Her cousin, sitting closest to the tangled garden of roses and other flowers, delicately situated a single orange impatiens bloom in the center of each leaf, completing the flowery meal with colorful "filling" on each "tortilla." The girls, attentive to their make-believe, talked quietly, busy making real in bright flowers, conversation, and gestures their imagined simple repast.

The girls were certainly not engaged in logic and discourse in making their tortilla supper. They are creating, as Susanne Langer (1982) might point out, a presentational symbol, "a simultaneous, integral presentation" of all the elements that make up their dinner—its visual aspects (the leaves, flowers, and plastic sheet), its dialogue (making and eating tortillas), and its actions (the patting of leaves, the placing of flowers, the careful display of the finished product at the front of the blue plastic square, like women displaying their wares in the market, or, perhaps, serving a meal at home on a *petate* or woven mat on the floor)—that make up its total structure. None of these elements has the same meaning as the entire sequence. The sense lies in the whole at once, in the "simultaneous, integral presentation" of flowers, leaves, actions, and quiet conversation.

This play, this presentational symbol, this enacted literature, has an additional significant and hidden center for the girls, a heart like the tiny ivory elephant inside a bright red Indian seed that discloses its meaning and magic simultaneously as the tiny ivory plug is removed, revealing the hidden animal inside. It is a narrative, a text of becoming and meaning, that lies in the vital center of play for the girls, and this narrative is necessary to connect each girl's ideas to the ideas of the other and sense and actions of the wider world (Paley, 1990). The girls create meaning for themselves that can be glimpsed by those around them as they engage in "the only set of circumstances understandable [by them] from beginning to end" (p. 6). This pretend meal, an image of gender roles and food preparation, the reenactment of daily events for Maya women, is similar to the traditional approach of the artist. In the carefully arranged shapes of leaves and flowers and in the soft dialogue of making a meal, the girls created their own idiosyncratic yet mutually intelligible meaning, engendering an image that serves as a link between them and their world. There is a circular pattern in this, a mutual reinforcing of images, stories, and social connections that brings us to the final connection of meaning and image where "the first thing we do with images is envision a story" (Langer, 1982, p. 145). As the Skin Horse might tell us, it is in the text of that story, in the forms of images, and in the connections with others that we create meaning, bestowing the designation of REAL on ourselves, our experiences, and the people in our lives.

Since images lead to narratives, and these show the way to the creation of individual and/or group meanings and to the creation of more representations, a further understanding of images and their sense-making capacities can be discovered in another play meal of two other little girls and the objects that they used to bring their repast to life.

Eight-year-old Amber and four-year-old Abigail busily shaped their modeling clay on the back porch of their family's home early one hot summer morning. They worked in silence except for an occasional request for materials—straws or toothpicks for drawing or poking—or the patting and thumping of clay. Amber, after several false starts, began an elaborate double-layered cake with a complex design on its top of incised lines and contrasting clay. Satisfied at last with the effect of the cake after the addition of toothpick candles with red clay flames, she began work on several small flat shapes, "cookies—cherry with chocolate chips—and brownies" as well as a large multicolored platter pounded flat with a meat mallet to hold her baked goods. Meanwhile, Abigail textured tiny flat clay shapes, adding more cookies to her sister's selection. The growing number of sweets appeared to give Amber another idea, for she began work on a fat brown teapot as a finishing touch for a tea party she intended to give during art time the following day (Kellman, 1995).

The next morning, with the temperature well into the 90s and the humidity not far behind, Amber began final preparations for the tea, undeterred by heat. She formed a hot dog on a bun, sliced it into three portions, and spread them with "mustard." Three tiny cups and saucers, a sugar bowl, and a creamer, created the night before, were placed strategically near the teapot. Much to Amber's dismay, Abigail, bored waiting for the party to begin and uninterested in making more pastries, consumed two "brownies" before anyone noticed. Satisfied with the last-minute details, Amber began to serve, passing out the hot dog, cookies, remaining brownies, and pouring out tea, making a "sh-hhhing" noise to indicate this activity. We sipped with similar sounds, making polite conversation between swallows as Amber blew out the candles and cut the cake. Then, as sudden as the appearance of a summer storm, the party was over, the food and tea consumed, everything returned to balls of clay except the cups, which Amber saved for another time.

This clay party, shared dialogue, and dramatic play, like the tortilla/leaf meal, is a two-person narrative, a story in which the girls created both their own and mutual meaning rich in imagery and full of continuing creative possibilities. The two meals are not only narratives, but also abstract images of individual and social roles and events, relating stories at the same time they form "primitive abstractions" for the children involved (Langer, 1982, p. 145). In the two enacted meals, this function of image as simple abstraction can be seen in the forms of the teapot and cake, the tortillas and filling, the accompanying imitated actions and stylized social conversations. The story (a symbol itself) arises from the entire play construct, for the meal encompasses the developing personae of four fictional adult women, the preparing and serving of food, and the performing of social interactions that such activities require in each of these two cultures. Such play and images can be understood as spontaneous descriptions of general ideas arising from the flow of impressions in the four girls' lives. They are descriptions of sociocultural forms related in actions, flowers, and clay by which the girls link themselves to one another and to their social worlds in "the only set of circumstances understandable by them from beginning to end" (Paley, 1990, p. 6), creating meaning for themselves and one another from the substance of their lives. Similarly, another young girl, seven-year-old Katie, whose autism was diagnosed before she was three, struggles to make sense of her experience through images of her world, a world composed of daily family activities and video cartoons portraying domestic interactions and silly adventures.

Katie helps to round out our examination of children with autism and their art, for she brings a distinctly female sensibility to an enterprise that, to this point at least, has been dominated by boys. Katie's imagery, like that of many little girls, includes the domestic sphere—scenes of both Daddy and Mommy brushing their teeth in a well-appointed bathroom (including soap, mirror, tissue box, and drinking glass); Katie waking up and stretching, still under the covers in her bed, her rabbit slippers waiting on the rug; a naked Katie, garments hanging behind her on a hook, dressing herself; her older brother at the beach and playing in the driveway of their home; her sister in bed; her smiling grandparents; and people seated at tables covered with dishes of steaming hot food. Even her fantasy characters—beguiling, toylike bears, rabbits, and pigs—seem to display little girls' more usual preoccupations with various emotional states and social interactions, domestic activities, and small-scale misadventures. When disorder does break out, it is no more terrible than an argument over an ice cream cone or an inadvertent collision with a cactus.

Katie takes her place with Jamie and Peter as an example of a talented young artist with autism for whom thinking in images is a critical activity, for she not only brings her own distinctive drawing preoccupations and purposes to our inquiries but also displays similarities in style and visual skill to one or the other or both of the boys. Like her male counterparts, she reveals in her drawings particular visual and graphic skills, characteristics that, as Sacks (1995) might agree, extend our "general understanding of intelligence and talent" and also perhaps "the vast realm that we now call the cognitive unconscious" (p. 194). To uncover these more complex layers of understanding, however, a brief description of Katie, her early history, and her art training are important.

KATIE

Katie's problems first appeared when she was about eighteen months old. However, her autism was not diagnosed until she was between three and three and a half years of age. During this same period of time Katie also became especially destructive, throwing frequent extended tantrums, breaking and shredding everything she could reach, screaming constantly, biting and hitting, and running ceaselessly—in circles around the perimeter of rooms when indoors or in any direction at all when outside. Additionally, she was unable to talk and slept and ate poorly. The family's difficulties during those "dark years," as Katie's mother calls them, eventually gave way under their tireless loving attention to Katie and her needs to her inclusion with an aide in a nearby public school kindergarten program. It was at this point that Katie's parents were finally able to shift some of their energies from the struggles of daily life to her education and to helping their daughter become part of the life of their community (Taylor, 1995a).

Katie's particular interest in Disney videos and her pleasure in arranging colors first appeared during her earliest, most difficult period, but it was not until kindergarten, when her teacher noticed her frequent drawing and doodling and her well-developed visual learning skills, that her family became aware of her special graphic abilities. To nurture Katie's newly discovered skills and to facilitate art's role as a possible means of communication and expression, her parents found an artist-teacher to tutor their daughter. Dennis Taylor, an art educator, was contacted at the same time to act as an adviser for the creation of art lessons appropriate to the special needs of a child with autism. It was at this point that Katie, lover of stuffed bears, possessor of Dolly the doll, owner of McDougall the cat, could be said to have begun her art career. By the time she was in first grade, much like Peter's parents, Katie's parents were able to imagine their daughter as a future Disney illustrator and to consider that the life of an artist would "tie into being her own personality." It was during this time, too, that Taylor began documenting Katie and her special skills (Taylor, 1995a).

My interest in Katie began two years later when I met Taylor at a conference, where we briefly discussed Katie and her art. I was at once intrigued. Here was a precocious young artist, a girl with autism who, like Peter, loved Disney studios. I wanted to know more about Katie and to see her drawings. A few weeks after I returned home from the conference, a thick envelope from Taylor arrived. As I hastily flipped through its contents, I was fascinated by what I saw, for page after page was covered by lively images showing the sure lines and complicated images of a girl with autism with clearly precocious art abilities. This virtuosity was itself an unusual occurrence, since girls with autism are less numerous than boys, and girls are more frequently profoundly affected. Katie, however, exhibited many similar drawing abilities to other young precocious, mainly male, artists with autism. Her skills, like these other artists, included exceptional observational abilities; tremendous rapidity and economy of line, and as a consequence, frequent use of fine-pointed drawing instruments, especially ballpoint pen or pencil; significant attention to visual structure; an exceptional skill in capturing motion; and an ability to render three-quarter, perspectival, foreshortened views that implied three-dimensional space. Additionally, like most other young artists with autism we have seen, Katie preferred to draw rather than use other less easily controlled art media. However, Katie, like Nadia, was apt to destroy her drawings as soon as she finished them (Taylor, 1995a). Nonetheless, Katie shared many familiar art-making characteristics with other young girls of her age without autism, too, especially a focus on the domestic and familial, on daily personal activities and social interactions, on clothes, and on descriptive details of garments and daily household clutter.

Katie the Artist

Katie, like all artists, has her own particular preoccupations of both subject and style. These include the use of a single energetic line to describe an image; particular attention to emotions—facial expressions, descriptive, active, quirky postures; description of interactions between figures; emphasis on details of elaborate figures and physical settings—animals' whiskers and patterns of fur, richly embellished garments; expressive teeth and mouths; eyes; and, in the best cartoon manner, a visual description of sounds—fierce, sharp lines to illustrate the barking of a dog, or jagged marks portraying the racket produced by two rabbits using jackhammers. Though Katie's interest in cartoons provides the subject matter for much of her art, so too, does her relationship with her close-knit family, another of Katie's distinctly personal considerations. Interspersed with the Berenstain Bears, the wacky frogs, buck-toothed rabbits, and tube-nosed pigs, one encounters drawings of her smiling grandparents, mother, father, brother, and sister engaged in familiar daily activities. In each case, family or cartoon, what Katie draws is a particular moment—a farmer rabbit gesturing at a spotted cow, a baby chick crowing as it hatches while its mother watches from her nest nearby, Katie's brother at the beach posed for a moment wearing trunks, an inner tube shaped like a snail, and a broad smile. It is this ability of Katie's to portray an arrested moment that gives her art some of its sense of immediacy and energy, for in this brief instant we see through Katie's eyes the scene that caught her attention in the first place. In the end it is with this idiosyncratic momentary perspective on the visual world of film or daily life that she charms us in brief descriptive lines.

This feeling of immediacy also suggests interpretations beyond the mere description of more concrete characteristics, for this vital sense ties Katie to the little girls we met earlier rehearsing social interactions and culturally grounded meal preparations as they explored the complexities of daily experience. Katie's drawings, whether in the form of cartoon animals or family pictures, appear to have the same deep need to rehearse or at least to mark—to portray the physical expressions of emotions and the actions that accompany them and to repeat what she has gleaned from both observation and experience of the daily world of work, play, pets, meals, school, and home. The cartoon characters come out of Katie's experience just as surely as the images of her family members do, for she is a devoted cartoon watcher; her finesse in drawing perspectival, three-quarter views in this video/movie-related format are as grounded in what she observes in these animated images as are her more obviously reality-based family drawings that come from her actual experience of daily events. At the same time, perhaps in a manner similar to the other little girls and their mimetic domesticity, Katie may be impelled toward her familial-based images by some awareness of female social roles as well as by her deep need for familiar recognizable structure and sense in her otherwise frequently difficult life.

Two particular drawings provide a means for exploring Katie's art as a whole, for between the solid realistic image of Daddy in the bathroom and the fanciful gathering of three squirrel-like creatures eating Popsicles in the company of a smaller squirrel dancing with what surely must be a pig, lie almost all of Katie's stylistic conventions and personal preoccupations. The drawing of Daddy in his shorts and athletic T-shirt is a good place to begin, for the visually based image of the bathroom fixtures that serve as her father's setting play a significant role, and Daddy himself is a charming mixture of observed and conceptualized characteristics, a figure knit together of what is seen, what is known, and what is most important to Katie.

The central portion of this drawing is marked off by the long rectangle of the vanity, which contains a semi-circular sink with curved faucet and rounded knobs. A tall mirror mounted with plastic clips hangs on the wall directly above the sink. Below the mirror and to its left, a soap dish with soap hovers above a transparent drinking glass on the vanity top below. Comb, hair dryer, and tooth-paste march left to right from wall to sink along the vanity's front edge. To the right of the basin the pace slows, for there is placed only a single container fol-lowed by the figure of Daddy himself lounging seal-like, his legs curved in a ninety-degree angle from his torso. Eyes wide, hair disheveled, his clubby three-finger hands extended stiffly from either side of his body, Katie's father reaches for the toothbrush in the wall holder beside him. An enormous toilet with a box with protruding tissue on its tank fills the floor to the right of the van-ity. The toilet, drawn with a minimum of continuous lines, provides an example of one of Katie's particular skills, for despite the toilet's apparent simplicity, it suggests foreshortening and perspective in a bold, economical manner.

Another aspect of Katie's rhythmic style, hastily applied color on individual objects that are evenly spread across the image—in this drawing, on soap, toothbrush, comb, hair dryer, toothpaste, container, father's hair, box of tis-sue, and toilet handle—is the slight obscuring of the forms of objects them-selves by the thick application of pigment. The rest of the bathroom drawing, like the toilet, is constructed in single, rapid lines that clearly describe the rela-tionship of objects in space and emphatically indicate the visual structure of the scene. The vanity, for example, utilizing foreshortening and perspective, stands away from the wall displaying a front and top surface and suggesting at the same time a far end near the toilet. The smaller objects, too, are similarly firmly located. The soap dish and toothbrush holder are both depicted in sweeping curves that move away from the implied wall in single rapid lines. The solid, semi-circular foreshortened container on the counter establishes a firm visual connection between Daddy and the sink. The vanity, drawn in a centrally located left-to-right direction, is clearly the result of visual observa-tion, for Katie is emphatic in her placement of objects and the perspectival characteristics of the fixtures themselves. No other objects are depicted above or below the central band of fixtures, however—another aspect of Katie's per-sonal approach to composition. From her first drawings in kindergarten to im-ages completed two years later, objects float in the center of her paper unencumbered by ground plane or additional images to either elaborate or an-chor the shapes beyond the central band. It is the figure of her father, however, around whom this composition revolves that is most interesting. Not only does Father hover over the vanity in a merman's posture, but he also is the last object at the end of the line of other objects at the same time that he forms the still center of the composition. A further quality that moves the viewer's eye directly to the figure of Daddy is his engaging air of startled surprise and peculiar forward-facing posture, which give him the appearance of someone who has suddenly been ejected from behind the vanity like a piece of toast from a toaster, only to discover the bathroom already occupied by both artist and viewer.

What might account for this drawing's rich mixture of careful details, three-dimensional attributes, and Father's unusual appearance? What might these qualities indicate about Katie? And how might this information form a link between Katie's struggle to find coherence and sense and the mutual social activities of the four girls at the beginning of this chapter?

Daddy, in his carefully described underwear, a curious figure made up of observed and conceptualized characteristics, forms the heart of the drawing and its various levels of meaning. He is both a thing among things lined up between the grooming items to his left and the Kleenex to his right, and a schema of Daddy, such as many other seven-year-old children draw—an unrealistic figure in a family bathroom reaching with bloated fingers for his toothbrush. This is not a visual report of a literal father except, perhaps, for his garments. The unusual pose tells us that. It is a figure based on Katie's concept of her father, like the earlier drawings by Tania of her father in heaven. Daddy's forward-facing posture as he rises from behind the vanity is a description of Katie's attention to what is significant for her about her father—his face, in this case, not his less expressive backside. To achieve this frontal view, Katie has rotated her father's figure 180 degrees from the usual wall-facing stance at a bathroom sink. At the same time, to include her father's entire body in the image (which she actually sees while he is in the bathroom), she has had to draw his legs strangely bent, rather than either tackling the logistical problem of her father on the wall side of the vanity (where, if in fact he were able to stand, his legs would not be seen at all) or being forced to draw his less important—to Katie, at least rear view. This is not to imply that Katie's drawing decisions were consciously thought out, but to indicate that this drawing illustrates in its compositional attributes an intermingling of cognitive operations. The figure of Daddy is both object and concept, a blending of what is seen and what is known in another way—Katie's sense of her father readying himself to brush his teeth in the three-dimensional visually based world of the bathroom.

Katie's visual engagement with the bathroom, the putting and placing of grooming implements, wall-mounted holders, mirror, toilet, and tissues, are as carefully and solidly situated as the leaf and flower tortillas lined up on the blue plastic sheet or the clay tea things on their small tray. Katie, like the other girls, demonstrates her knowledge, visual and otherwise, of a small portion of her domestic world, of the place and role of particular objects, and the expected interactions with them. At the same time, though Katie herself is not enacting a social event with another child, she is nonetheless making a thorough report of her father's activities in front of the vanity, knitting together, like Amber, Abigail, and Rosa and her cousin, her internal and external experience in the mixture of visual and conceptual qualities in her drawing.

Katie's second image, labeled "Leahtel lime popscicles for lurch" by two wavering lines of print across the top, contains not only evidence of her abiding interest in video cartoons but also several of her other most frequently used drawing ploys. Like her drawing of her father, for example, this image of gleeful animals eating Popsicles also begins on the left with the tail of a small-profile rodent (a squirrel, perhaps) seated in a high-backed chair with a sweet in its paw and ends with a record player with hovering musical notes on a small square cabinet on the right margin of the paper. In between, two larger Popsicle-eating animals in tall chairs face the viewer from the far side of a long table, repeating the now familiar centrally placed rectangular schema. The larger rodent on the left, unlike his companions, has neither legs nor chair below the tabletop. A half-hidden, bow-bedecked grinning pig capers with the smallest rodent in front of the record cabinet on the far right of the image. All the animals wear shirts, pants, and shoes, and except for the pig, whose eyes are hidden, all have large oval eyes with pupils rolled to the left, as do most of Katie's other creatures. Even the *O* in "for" has been turned into an eye with a left-looking pupil, indicating not only Katie's attention to goofy details but an additional item from her stock of conventionalized, schematic forms. The "lurch" drawing is completed by a three-quarter perspectival image of what appears to be a shoe box lying in the center foreground, for two footprints are outlined on its left side. This unexpected three-dimensional object adds a satisfying triangular shape to the composition as a whole by providing an apex for the wider, thicker band of animals and letters above it.

Not all is undiluted joy in "popscicles for lurch," however, for the middle rodent is not smiling. This animal, one hand on its right hip and the left holding a sweet to his snarling mouth, appears to be outraged. His brows are beetled and his teeth are showing, providing a perfect example of Katie's second-most frequent choice of expression after her usual smiling faces. In this drawing as in her other art, Katie's energetic, continuous line not only describes the major forms but picks out the details—foxy tail tips, waists, sleeves, pants bottoms, and gridlike teeth, and even separate smaller heel marks on the footprints on the foreground box, as if to indicate pumps. Katie's characteristic use of hue applied on evenly spaced, single objects also helps to emphasize details, in the "lurch" drawing: a tail, two Popsicles, and the arm of the record player. This rather diffuse use of color, as is true in so many of Katie's other drawings, is employed at evenly spaced intervals that emphasize the horizontal quality of her composition. Thus, the "lurch" image, like the bathroom scene, also exhibits her frequent preference for a structure that is largely horizontal, always without a literal baseline with wide bands of empty paper on either side of a central strip of images, and made up of expressive, detailed characters in one domestic setting or another.

Katie's preference for homey images of her family and of her beloved cartoon creatures creates a continuously running narrative that mingles what Katie sees with what she knows, what she experiences herself and what she observes in a video. It is this literally and virtually experienced domestic narrative that Katie explores in her drawings as she investigates in what order a day unrolls, in what shape a week proceeds, in what way people act and interact within the shelter of family and friends. Katie unites her interior and exterior life in these closely observed drawings in a seeable narrative in which she surely makes some sense of her world at the same time she charms us with her fanciful giggling creatures and ingratiating, smiling family.

Even though Katie spends much of her time on domestic imagery, she nonetheless shares a number of art-making characteristics with Jamie and Peter, whose subjects take very different directions. One quality all three children possess is their ability to create images firmly grounded in what they see—in cartoons and movies, and, to a lesser extent, in their own lives. Just as Jamie prefers action movies such as *The Towering Inferno*, Peter's interest lies in *The Wizard of Oz*, and Katie loves the Berenstain Bears. The impersonal, visually engaging format of video with vigorous action, infinitely repeatable scenes, and a dependable cast of characters provide the subjects for these young artists' art by presenting images that satisfy their particular interests. These interests include such diverse topics as architecture and autos, fairy tales and tornadoes, and domestic adventures and slapstick silliness. This material allows these three young artists not only to repeat their favorite scenes by rerunning the video itself, but also to explore each visible nuance, every shift in light and composition for as long as they wish by simply stopping the video on a particular frame. At the same time, the videos allow these children to draw what they see without the bothersome qualities of personal interactions and the jarring messiness of daily life intruding into their purely visual experience.

These young artists are alike in other, more specifically drawing-related ways, too. Perhaps the most obvious similarity is the fact that they all rely on line, energetic and unambiguous, to create most of their drawings. This preference for line as a particularly important compositional element is understandable in the light of both the initial qualities of the visual process itself and the children's particular drawing preoccupations, for their visual interests are best and most clearly stated in specifically linear terms. Other shared drawing characteristics, all grounded in the clear sight of unobscured visual processes and unclouded by conceptual considerations include emphasis on outline and surface details; special attention to the three-dimensional qualities of foreshortening and perspective; focus on the *structure* of visual scenes; hue as a purely structural, additive element; and the active, expressive qualities of images.

It is perhaps the case that this latter characteristic may also be influenced by the fact that people's vision is arrested as our eyes move to follow motions or to scan an image, and it is the brain that strings them into a seamless view describing action (Burr, Morrone, & Ross, 1994). At the same time, video and movie images themselves are a series of single frames strung together to create the moving image. Thus, it is possible that the characteristics of the way people see and the nature of film itself further enable these exceptionally clear-eyed young artists to catch an instant in time on a piece of paper—a spoon caught just in front of an animal's mouth, a car forever poised halfway over a cliff, the Tin Man halted midstride. At the same time, of course, that the nature of the vision process provides an explanation for the compositional characteristics themselves, these elements in their turn make the use of fine-pointed drawing instruments necessary to achieve their particular qualities.

One last small but interesting characteristic that all three young artists share not only with one another but with many other artists with autism is a sharp eye for the presence of electrical plugs, wall sockets, electrical cords, appliances, and light fixtures as important elements in a drawing. For example, in Peter's drawing, "The Queen of Makeup" (who we will meet later), he has drawn the hairdryer with a plug and wall socket at least as large as the dryer itself (see Figure 6.1); similarly, Katie has drawn a popcorn maker with a plug and three-hole receptor wall socket the size of the head of one of the main figures in that same image. Though this is one of Katie's few involvements with electrical equipment, her placement of the carefully drawn giant plug and socket as the highest, nearly central objects in her image, links her, to Jamie's special attention to wiring in many of his architectural drawings, as well as to Peter and the queen's hair dryer.

However alike these young artists are in many ways—from the source of much inspiration in videos to their precocious, visually based drawing skills that provide a particular approach to image making—there are interesting and informative differences in subject matter, drawing skills, and styles that suggest significant qualities of each young artist's creations. For example, though Katie and Peter share a preoccupation with chubby, charming Disney cartoon characters, Katie's attention is particularly on the actions, interactions, and expressive characteristics of her figures, whereas Peter renders his subjects with a sure line that emphasizes their solid physical characteristics more than their social and/or emotional attributes. Jamie, however, provides his own series of examples, for his images are more carefully done than those by Peter or Katie as

Figure 6.1
The Queen of Makeup, Peter, age eight, marker on paper

befits a budding architect, and he most frequently grapples with the object as a three-dimensional form rather than exploring its other qualities. Jamie's images, gleaned from moments of chaos in action pictures, are carefully drawn descriptions of objects in space, an architectural view of fistfights, broken furniture, and car wrecks. By contrast, if Katie can be said to imply space, absorbed as she is by action and emotional weather, it can be said that Jamie investigates it in detail, running his pencil over the rise and fall of each visible surface, determining the degrees of an angle, describing the exact spatial relationship of objects and forms.

Just as Katie and Jamie seem to represent seemingly opposite positions in regard to subject choice and compositional concerns, so, too, they exhibit anticipated culturally described differences between boys' and girls' art making. For example, Katie, with apparent interest in clothing and its details, domestic activities, and emotional responses of cute cartoon animals is not unlike many other girls her age, whereas Jamie's interest in automobiles, car chases, and di-

sasters is not unlike other boys' interests in second grade. Peter's images, however, place him outside this usual classroom gender-based dichotomy, for
children ever attentive to magic dust, fairies, and lurking mice in a world
touched by the Magic Kingdom are frequently little girls.

Katie's mingling of explorations of fantasy, family, and small domestic concerns bring to mind investigations of Abigail, who similarly begins her imagery
firmly grounded in the experience of the family celebrations but shifts into fantasy in the final elaboration of her clay sculpture. This apparent resemblance
between the two girls is important, for it not only underscores Katie's resemblance to other girls her age, but also suggests the possibility that she engages
in a more complicated activity than simple reportage when she draws. To see
this same amalgam of the fantastic with the mundane in the art of Abigail, a
child artist without autism, we must return to the back porch before the tea
party where we met her earlier and watch her create something with this mixture of domesticity and make-believe.

While her older sister worked on her cake and candles for the upcoming tea
party, Abigail, too, formed a cake, a flat red and green disk, hamburgerlike in
size and shape, incised with designs drawn with a toothpick. Soon the disk became a forest, however, with four bundles of toothpicks pressed into its surface
at equal intervals, leaving its central area empty. "People dance in the middle of
the forest," Abigail announced, "with chickens. White chickens. No little yellow baby chicks." This cake-forest-dancing-people-poultry patty, first an image and then a story, is also a fine example of image making as a mode of
untutored thinking and stories as its earliest outcome. The enchanted patty
grew out of the exploration of clay by Abigail as she prodded, poked, pounded,
and shaped her materials to create a form that became, in the end, a forest with
human and avian dancers, a simultaneous place and narrative that leads us to
our original discussion of the child's struggle to comprehend the nature of being, the effort to establish a viable self, and the complexities of developing a
sustainable, coherent, social world. This is the business of life, and all children,
even those with autism in their own deeply idiosyncratic manner, are engaged
in this undertaking. We have seen that just as surely as images lead to stories,
stories themselves lead to at least some sort of meaning and sense, however
personal. We have discovered that art develops from the interior life being
brought forward into exterior experience. Finally, we have seen in the art of
Peter, Jamie, and Katie how precocious young artists with autism set about
their efforts at meaning making in the visual language of structure, line, form,
and three-dimensional qualities.

But what of children with autism who are in no way precocious but make
art? How do they fit into our understanding of art as text, as an integrative activity, as a way to create sense for one's self, and as a deeply meaningful activity

where making real becomes a possibility? Mark, the only child of two engineers and a member of a special classroom in a public school near his home, enjoys art making but is in no way precocious. He will be our exemplar here, for though he is not a prodigy, Mark is in every way a creative young man.

MARK

It was the Christmas holiday and Mark, a soft, round boy looking younger than his eleven years, was still in his pajamas though his thick brown hair was neatly combed. Perched like an enormous, bright colored baby bird on the top bunk, backlit by the sun that poured through the window behind him, Mark seemed nervous and curious both as he carefully took in my arrival with his parents in quick sideways glances. I placed my art supplies on a small, desklike sewing machine—a stack of paper, a collection of fine-line markers, graphite pencils, ballpoint pens. Mark spied them instantly, and as soon as we adults began to chat among ourselves, he crept off his high seat to investigate. In a minute or two and with little prompting from his parents, Mark sat down to draw, perhaps partially enticed by the presence of markers since his mother does not let him use them at home to save herself the misery of stained clothing in the laundry. Whatever the reason for his interest, however, Mark eagerly churned through a dozen and a half pieces of paper in the space of twenty-five minutes, grabbing a new sheet as soon as he completed each image, charging through a series of drawings with total absorption in his task, his nose only inches from his images.

This drawing posture of Mark's is of particular interest, for he draws with his head on his arm, observing his creations from inches away and placing himself as closely as possible to the center of the action. Holding a pencil or marker loosely between his thumb and all four fingers of his right hand, Mark seems to flick his drawing instrument at the paper. Even with this seemingly desultory approach, however, Mark is able to achieve a surprising degree of control, for his vigorous images rapidly grow from the dense tangle of lines created by this casual technique and develop from the central structures of highly gestural, linear elements. As he draws, Mark also produces sound effects for the action in the images as well as occasional snatches of dialogue and shouted commands, apparently living the action in the worlds that he creates while he brings them into being. Mark, it seems, is not drawing scenelike illustrations in the usual child artist's perspective as a close eye-level observer; he is drawing the actions themselves, portraying the linear structure of activities taking place on his sheet of paper as if they were in process before him, describing explosions, tracing trajectories, following the path of travel of energetic lines, and producing the dense, snarly bodies of whirling planets and spaceships.

It is this structural, action-based quality of images that serves as the key to the rest of Mark's art, for it brings us directly to the central issues of his drawings—a gestural examination of solid forms, an investigation into relationships among the visual structures of actions and of shapes in motion, the development of narratives from a core of visual events, and the insistence on the fundamental role of written and spoken words as part of the graphic experience. Granted, these are not drawing preoccupations that Mark could either name or describe, but they are, nonetheless, the qualities he repeatedly investigates on the surface of his paper. To see why these drawing qualities are central, related, and of value in gaining insight into Mark himself, we must turn briefly to Mark's early childhood and follow his story forward to Mark as he is now, as he stands at the beginning of puberty and adolescence.

Even Mark's earliest creations employ both the gestural examination of forms and the visual complexities of motion, two significant drawing concerns that, as we have discovered, he continues to explore even now, years later, in both two- and three-dimensional art. For example, as a four-year-old, his alphabet drawings and his book of ratty tape and mixed paper titled "Little Nemo and the Two Girls" already contained these traits. In his image "X x" from this early alphabet series, the central figure is built up of heavy layers of repeated graphite marks that follow the direction of each body part's physical structure—the legs from short hasty, vertical lines, the torso from a diminishing series of ever smaller squares, and the head from an even smaller set of nested notations. The drawing is completed by a series of colored stickers—a smiling boy's head, two hearts, and an x-ray view of a foot and arm that form the face and torso, two large hands that suggest the arms, and a large yellow pencil, which seems to serve as the penis. Even though it is partially obscured by stickers, the figure's original composition is clearly gestural, for it is made up of rapid, repeated lines that imply, rather than distinctly describe, the vigorous body of a boy being X-rayed. Similarly, in the book "Little Nemo and the Two Girls," the figures are drawn in wiry rapid scribbles that initially tangle together to indicate the girls' hair and Nemo's hat, then slow into single short curves for the figures' mouths, and finally tighten into hasty, expressive circles for eyes. Throughout his book, bodies and appendages are frequently drawn with a single line following the exterior limits of the forms themselves, outlining the rectangular shapes of legs and arms, the half ellipse forms of fingers, the nearly circular heads—as if the bodies had been created by Dr. Frankenstein from a previously assembled stock of predictable parts. Nonetheless, even in these early, less action-oriented images, a feeling of motion pervades Mark's drawings in a manner reminiscent of Katie's art, for it seems that he, like Katie, is intent on the quick flicker of a facial expression and the ceaseless small motions of a living body and is able to deftly catch them in his drawings. "Little Nemo and the Two Girls" is not just an example of lively linearity, however, for it is also an early example of another of Mark's continuing drawing preoccupations—the development of narrative from visual events. These images are arranged into a short book complete with cover and carefully lettered title, a clear reference to at least some of the conventions of other printed stories and tales. At the same time, it is this mixture of image and print on Little Nemo's cover that brings us to the final continuing theme in both Mark's life and art. The use of words is not only found in the creation of visual narratives, but also encountered as an embellishment in other drawings and three-dimensional work, and as a decorative element in his bedroom.

This frequent use of language in visual creations is particularly interesting, for Mark, who did not begin to talk until he was eight (first with nouns, then later with pronouns, according to his mother), does not usually use complete sentences even now, though when angry, he is apt to utter entire sentences without hesitation. Usually, Mark is echolalic, repeating words, sounds, and sentence fragments. His repertoire includes sound effects from videos and computer games; dialogue from cartoons and movies, particularly *Star Trek* adventures; advertising slogans; tsk-tsk noises; and pieces of sentences from books and commercial texts. Despite Mark's current inability to use language comfortably, his engagement with spoken and written language began early, leading his grandparents, at least, to wonder if he might be a genius. At the age of one and a half he could say the alphabet backward and forward, and at the age of two he began to read, though without comprehension.

At the same time, during Mark's early childhood, the alphabet seemed to serve as a particular means of providing comfort and structure. One notable example is particularly touching: When Mark was less than two and left with his grandparents for even a short period of time, he would stand at the back door reciting the alphabet forward and backward, as if the letters themselves brought him relief from his anxiety of seeing his parents drive off. The use of words as possible creators or markers of safe space can even now perhaps be seen in Mark's insistence that over his bedroom door there should hang (as there has for years) a sign reading THE END, and recently, Mark's mother has discovered the same phrase inscribed on the wall next to his bed, a possible additional sign or source of comfort.

This interest in signs, titles, letters, and words displayed so frequently in Mark's art is demonstrated by phrases and sound effects hovering over the action in his drawings, names and numbers on rockets and space vehicles, and titles of books, videos, or other culturally provided images of one sort or another in bold letters on many of his creations. The drawing series "Colony Alert" provides an excellent example of both Mark's comic book–style inclusion of dialogue on drawings and his vigorous, intimate engagement with the action in the drawings themselves.

Completed while his parents and I sit nearby, this series of seventeen marker and graphite drawings begins with a kumquat-sized orange ball in the center of the first sheet of paper, moves with increasing compositional density to elaborate images of whirling green planets and long-tailed comets, half-page sinister hemispheres of black distant worlds, starships and satellites engaged in combat, and guns tracing vigorous marks across the white paper of space, and concludes with Mark's familiar gestural figures seated in what surely must represent cockpits. In three of the last drawings, figures shrink to insignificant black scribbles on an increasingly damaged planet, diminished, it seems, by the fearsome barrage from space. The pace of the drawing also accelerates throughout the series so that the density and energy of marks, the number of images and hues, and the inclusion of sound effects—"Dooooooom! KAKA! Thooooooor! Adooom! Kaboom!"—increase throughout, only to taper off in the final three drawings to silence and lessening visual complexity. At the height of the battle, words elaborate two of the drawings as figures shout, "Fire!" and "Colony Alert." At the same time, the viewer's perspective shifts from a position far out in space and distant from the action to the intense middle drawings, where spaceship cockpits or colony dwellings elaborate the foreground along with the figures themselves. Distance asserts itself as the battle fades in the final images and the viewer is again in space looking back at the exploding planet. This far, near, far perspective on the action, coupled with a similar repetition of simple, complex, simple in the density of composition in the images themselves provides a visual richness to the series of drawings and a natural rhythm and narrative pattern to the images as a whole.

Mark's vigorous personal engagement with the drawing process itself further suggests the possibility of narrative being embedded in the visual events of his images, and at the same time, his behavior demonstrates and enacts the complex relationship between rapid, cumulative mark making, vigorous action, and the importance of spoken and written words in his art. Sounding as if he were repeating a script he has previously heard (which may be the case), Mark uses not only words but also apparently their previously encountered intonations throughout the drawing process. "Going down! Going down!" "Red alert! Red alert!" "Purple alert! Purple alert!" "Oh, my God! Oh, my God! Oh, my God! Not so fast, Kang!" "Eyes of Terror!" "You will enter mine!" "Now you are a repfile [sic]!" And finally, "Colony alert! Colony alert!" Tongue clicks, hums, and a long, deep bell-like tone suggesting a movie soundtrack composed to describe deep space or perhaps to imitate the sound of distant chanting Tibetan monks also accompany the shouted warnings and commands. It is as if Mark himself were taking part in the invasion, for each hastily snatched piece of paper seems to indicate his own changing perspective as a viewer moving with various scenes flashing before his eyes as the action advances through time and space. Even the cannon fire has both auditory and visual results as the sound of detonating shells accompanies the glowing orange, graphite, and yellow trajectories that rise and fall across the surface of the devastated planet.

Mark's drawings bring into being a universe in the midst of action, a real and experiential world in which he seems to take part as he creates it. Based on his favorite video and computer images and likely influenced by his father's work on rockets and rocket fuel for NASA and his own experiences with his father seeing real rockets in various displays and exhibits, Mark's space vehicles and stations have a vigorous physical presence and sense of immediacy from the moment he begins to bring them into being. His focus is on the actual, on the flow of time and experience itself as evidenced by the large number of cutout images he produces, for it is usual for Mark to use his scissors to shape his rockets after he has finished drawing them, turning them into individual physical objects instead of elements in a drawing. Two particular paper figures are of special interest, for they contain most of the motifs that appear in Mark's other shaped drawings, though they do not include letters, numbers, or words or the floating title of a movie drifting behind them, like many of his other creations.

The first image, the flight deck of a spaceship drawn as if one were standing behind the brown-haired pilot and co-pilot and peering with them through the three raggedly cut-out windows at the action beyond, may, according to his parents, refer to an image first seen in a computer space adventure where the action takes place beyond the window openings. Drawn with a mixture of crayon and pencil, the cockpit is depicted with a black floor, two Prussian blue seats on either side of a central gray control assembly, and a graphite and orange front wall opening into the emptiness of space itself. Built up of repeated, rapid, gestural marks in thick layers of crayon and pencil, the cockpit shimmers with the energy generated by these multiple vigorous lines. It is this energy and the quirky open windows that pull the viewer into the action, placing him/her directly in the center of the adventure as the spaceship swoops on its unknown mission.

The second image also encompasses particular qualities that are in evidence throughout Mark's cutout drawings, for it combines his interest in rocketry, penchant for making images as realistic as possible, and his warm relationship with his father. This drawing, also a combination of media like most of his other art, is done in ballpoint pen, pencil, and crayon. The main form has been lightly sketched in by Mark's father at the boy's request, a not infrequent strategy in some of Mark's art. After his father completed the outline, Mark, as he has done in several other drawings, colored the image and inserted the details he felt were vital. The slender star fighter with elongated gunlike snout, thin wings, and delicate protrusions of equipment and stabilizers of a variety of sorts, is lightly colored green in front and yellow in back with bright red scribble balls marking the cockpit, midwings, and left wing tip. What resembles a radar attachment rising behind the cockpit is emphasized in bright, solid spring green. Two service vehicles or perhaps attacking ships done in ballpoint pen are adhered to the fighter with glue or tape. A small, stubby rocket clings to the rear of the fighter. A larger, more complex ball-shaped rocket bridges the space between the right wing and its forward fuselage. Like Mark's other images, the fighter is formed with rapid, repeated gestural lines, which imply shape at the same time they suggest volume and motion. It seems that Mark made as real as possible his vision of a rocket at the same time he engaged in a mutually satisfying activity with his father.

Closely related to the detailed, realistic rendering and the objectlike quality found in the cutout images are Mark's refurbished boxes in a variety of styles. Using castoff household cartons as a starting point (frequently software and model containers), Mark glues drawings to their exterior surfaces to give them new life as his own imagined software, books, and games. In a similar additive manner, he alters his parent's models of rockets to his own taste by adhering additional paper details. These include fuel tanks, identification letters, and numbers, which make the models conform to his idea of the physical appearance of real rockets. In a related attempt at realism in which actual objects mingle with his own creations, Mark has piled cardboard boxes in his room to create display shelves like those that belong to his parents, placing in the pasteboard containers his own toy models of rockets, one rocket to a box, to show off the space vehicles to best advantage. Even in his collecting, box-stacking activities Mark is linked to other children's creative enactments and play, for his behavior is in no way different from other children's concoctions and constructions. His shelves similarly include a variety of materials to replicate the look of familiar adult behavior and belongings, perhaps for a moment, at least, attempting "the business of making meaning," as Hubbard (1989) and Paley (1990) might agree.

It is possible that all of Mark's multifaceted calling into being through images, objects, words, and sounds, his making real with scissors and glue, can be seen to link him to other children and their imaginative undertakings with whatever comes to hand—flowers and clay, leaves and sticks, bits of fabric and paper, and other items that make up the *bricolage* of children's creative undertakings. Nearly all children are natural *bricoleurs*, using the stuff they encounter in their world as the raw material for breathing life into the interactions, actual, imagined, or culturally provided, in which they take part. It is not unlikely that Mark, like so many other children, in his own way rehearses, repeats, and constructs his personal narratives in a similar rich mixture of fragments from his family's life, creating a body of images "in terms of which his life makes sense" (Bellah, Madsen, Sullivan, Swindler, & Tipton, 1985).

We have seen, however, that as Mark makes real the space adventures that embroider his life, he also shares the now familiar drawing strategies and compositional characteristics with Jamie, Peter, and Katie: Mark, too, describes the elements found in the process of seeing. We have discovered that Mark's drawings, like the art of these three children, employ rapid, wiry lines to create spatially grounded structures, indicate motion, and describe a consistent three-dimensional emphasis. And as might be expected, Mark, who is by no means a virtuoso nor as interested in art as the other children, has even developed a preference for fine-pointed drawing tools to create his drawings.

To clarify how Mark's creations relate to the drawings of these other, more skilled young artists with autism, however, further comparisons and contradistinctions between his drawings and those of the others is called for; such an undertaking allows us not only to see him as exhibiting many similar drawing characteristics to these children, but also suggests that what we discover is characteristic of the visual skills of exceptional young artists with autism and perhaps characteristic of the particular manner in which many children with autism envision their world.

As before, Jamie the young architect will begin our discussion, for in many ways he still remains satisfyingly emblematic of the other young artists we have examined. His art exemplifies not only the many drawing characteristics these children share, and his interest in particular movies heralds the same sort of visual and narrative preoccupations found in the lives and art of Katie, Peter, and Mark. As we consider Mark in relation to Jamie and the other children, however, it is necessary to recall what we have learned about him previously and to describe how unlike these other young artists he is in several important ways. First, Mark is four years older than the other children. Second, like Katie but unlike Peter and Jamie, he does not talk frequently or fluently. Third, again like Katie but unlike Peter and Jamie, his early years were marked by angry tantrums and destructive behavior. Fourth, unlike either of the two younger boys, Mark even now requires a constant companion to keep him from wandering away or getting into difficulty. Fifth, and finally, though Mark likes art and has begun to attempt computer graphics, his parents have not, at least until this new interest developed, imagined him becoming a professional artist, and he has never been considered an extraordinarily artistic child in the same manner that Jamie, Peter, and Katie have been.

It is easy for us to recall Jamie and his sweeping panoramas of the beach cottage, gridlock traffic jams, and numerous *Towering Inferno* drawings, for his sure, single line, drawn without a ruler, carefully describes each aspect of complicated buildings with rich interior details, automobiles and engines, and the many scenes of chaos, collapse, and decay caused by stupendous car wrecks, conflagration, urban blight, and fistfights. With his solid, vigorous line, Jamie implies space, describes foreshortening, and explains spatial relationships, and it is with this line that he brings energy and verve to his structurally focused drawings. Stories gleaned from adventure movies serve as important sources for many of Jamie's drawings, but so, too, do his daily personal experiences. In his rich amalgam of the actual and virtual, the local and exotic, of yesterday, to-day, and last summer, Jamie, we have seen, is able to create a personal narrative that contains meaning and sense, especially for himself. In the end, we have come to understand that Jamie spins meaning from the rich material provided by his acute visual processes and complex visual memory. It is this apparent at-tempt to engender such meaning that underlies much of his art. In a similar manner to Jamie, Mark, as we have discovered, explores material from his own life—his parents' Little Nemo comics, rocket models, computer games, family favorite space videos, and even his father's job—in his drawings of rockets and space vehicles, interplanetary struggles, software and game graphics, and even his early production "Little Nemo and the Two Girls." Unlike Jamie's detailed drawings of a family vacation dwelling, Mark seems to stick to other-world ad-ventures drawn from his family's favorite pastimes and professional interests to the exclusion of other, more domestic subjects.

It is most clearly in the use of particular drawing elements and strategies and in the visually based quality of his drawings that Mark, like Jamie (and Peter and Katie, too), sets himself off from children without autism whose art fre-quently concentrates on concepts and sociocultural constructs rather than vi-sually based linear descriptions of images and their disposition in space. It is this linear investigation of three-dimensional visual structures and the orienta-tion and spatial location of objects, implied rather than stated in Mark's rather hasty style, that provides his many cutout drawings with a feeling of unex-pected vitality based on what certainly seems to be acute visual observation. At the same time, Mark's particularly vigorous line appears to suggest the art of yet another well-known virtuoso young artist with autism in its motion-cap-turing rapidity. His line, though less precise than Nadia's and used to build up, not outline form, links his art to hers in its vigorous gestural implication of both form and movement.

However, it is not only drawing characteristics but Mark's unambiguous engagement with making real that returns us to our initial consideration of Katie, Jamie, and Peter and the many other precocious young artists with au-tism who also create visual and narrative sense and meaning in their art. It is as a visual teller of tales, a *bricoleur* of household materials, a visual librarian of fam-ily interests, and a small idiosyncratic Orpheus singing into being the very actions of a world, that Mark is tied most closely to the deep, hot visual heart of the three other young creators' lives. It is from the similar shared complex mixture of personal and family experiences, socially provided tales, preferences, art-making materials, and unobscured visual capacities that Mark's own individual narrative meanings are developed and become comprehensible even in their most idiosyncratic qualities, and, at the same time, become finally most like the art and play found in other children's lives.

A final story assures us of similar creative features in the experiences of two other children. It is a short tale of two girls of about nine, skipping through the sun-dappled shade with the mother of one of them. As I walked passed the little group, I overheard one child ask, "Hey, Mom, when Audrey and me get home, can we tape two stars on a stick to make a wand?" I thought about this small request later, and it occurred to me the girls would be doing several things at once as they worked on their wand. They would be composing an image, sharing a story, devising mutual meaning, and bringing into the world what they know of enchantment and of being together on a mild summer morning. In this mutual act, the girls would be formulating their social selves with the magic of their wand and the narrative that would give it life. The girls would be making the wand as genuine as possible, like Mark and his father and their careful paper rockets, and the girls, too, would become real to each other in the shared story of their briefly merged lives.

7

Current Research: Directions and Suggestions

Since the first descriptions of autism as a distinct disorder by Kanner in 1943 and the clarification of the classical triad of deficits at least thirty years ago, research and clinical inquiry into the causes of autism have taken several directions. One avenue of both research and clinical investigation has begun with the individuals themselves—those who exhibit the diagnostic triad of characteristics, which includes deficits of reciprocal social relationships, communication, and imagination. These are often accompanied by the curious combination of nontriadic signs that are commonly cited but are not essential to the diagnosis of autism: abnormal responses to sensory stimuli, preoccupations with parts of objects, savant abilities, and idiosyncratic peaks in perceptive and visuospacial functioning (Frith & Happé, 1994). Thus, with the individual as a starting point, research and clinical studies have questioned the implications and possible sources of such characteristics in genetic inheritance, brain functioning and structure, biochemical processes, and specific qualities and processes of mind and behavior.

Other inquiries have focused on the family and its context, questioning the relationship and interaction of genetic and personal characteristics of various family members to one another, to their environment, and to the syndrome of autism. Twin, sibling, parent-child, and, when possible, multigenerational studies, as well as examinations of related physiological characteristics and behaviors, have been described and statistically explained. Still other inquiries have employed literature reviews and comparisons of research as a source for additional information and possible hypothesis. These studies and innumerable others have led to the continuing interplay between research and clinical work that make up the inquiries into autism today. Researchers continue to grapple with this disorder, which for the most part still cannot be said to have an identifiable cause, though chromosomal abnormalities, metabolic disorders, and infectious agents have all been implicated (Ghaziuddin & Burmeister, 1999).

In the late 1990s and early 2000, however, the most exciting research into the etiology of autism is provided by molecular genetics, which, through a combination of technological and conceptual advances, has made it possible to localize likely susceptible genes for psychiatric disorders and potentially to identify the particular genes involved in the disorder of autism, too. The successful discovery of such genes (for it is certain no one gene is responsible here) will likely come in the next ten years, according to some researchers (Rutter, 1999). The identification of responsible genes will finally lead to the research necessary to determine the functional consequence of such genes and "will make a real difference to the power to determine the neural process involved in the causation of autism" (p. 181). At the same time, the future integration of clinical, genetic, neuropsychological, and neurobiological perspectives on the autistic syndrome will, it is hoped, finally come about, thereby creating a perspective on the disorder that will make sense of even its most baffling manifestations. These discoveries and others, too, will at last make it possible to devise methods of both prevention and intervention that offer the families of children with autism the first clearly defined and well-understood series of treatment and preventive options since the disorder was initially described.

To discover what such research might suggest for the young artists with autism we have met, an examination of a portion of current research will be useful. We will begin with the recognition of the growing general interest in the disorder, for within the last few years autism has become a more publicly visible condition, and the dialogue about the syndrome is no longer only between researchers, doctors, and the families of children who have autism.

Examples of autism's current higher profile can be seen in the substantial number of professional journals dedicated to the disorder itself and in the growing number of papers on autism in scholarly journals on related topics. The publications on autism have also expanded to include autobiographical accounts of general interest by people with autism such as writer and researcher Temple Grandin (1995b) and biographical articles and stories of personal reflections on experiences such as those by noted neurologist and writer Oliver Sacks (1995). At the same time, television programs by and about families of children with autism, presentations on the syndrome itself, interviews with adults with autism, articles in popular magazines, and radio specials have all undertaken descriptions and explanations of autism, its effect on people and their families, and the current state of research on the disorder.

This widening, more public discussion of the syndrome has not only increased awareness of autism itself, but also has led to a more general interest in its causes and in hopes for future management strategies. A recent article by professor of obstetrics and gynecology Patricia Rodier (2000) is an example of just such an individual awakening to the subject of autism and its profound effects on individuals with the disorder. Since Rodier also is an embryologist who previously focused on birth defects of the brain with a particular interest in injuries to the developing fetal nervous system, she began her current research into autism after noticing its unusually high frequency in children who have suffered from prenatal thalidomide damage. Because of her prior training, this apparent linkage of thalidomide to autism suggested to her the possibility of pinpointing autism's origins in the early malformation of a developing fetus. Rodier's description of her growing interest and insight and of her eventual hypothesis regarding the origin of autism in early fetal growth will serve as a framework for our own investigations into current research on autism and its causes. We will start our inquiry with what is certainly the beginning of the story of autism itself as well as the questions that surround its appearance—the prenatal and perinatal factors that appear to influence the development of autism. Then, we will briefly touch on genetics, embryology, and neurobiology, on the physical and cognitive markers of autism, and finally, on the variety of hypotheses that have been advanced in regard to each. In the end, we will return to the children themselves, giving our attention again to our small, artistically precocious companions and the marks they make that both record and elaborate their lives.

RISK FACTORS, CHROMOSOMES, AND GENES

Since little is known regarding the possible risk factors associated with autism, a group of researchers in North Dakota set out to at least suggest which social/familial factors might accompany the syndrome in an attempt to address the problem from the point of view of public health and family counseling (Burd, Severud, Kerbeshian, & Klug, 1999). By matching the names of patients who met the criteria for autism and autistic disorder with their birth certificates, the researchers were able to identify seven possible risk factors among the seventy-eight people with the disorder in contrast to the 390 individuals who served as controls. After removing two factors to account for unreliable results, the researchers were left with five variables in their final model of presumed risks.

These variables include an array of factors—decreased birth weight, low maternal education, late start of prenatal care, and a previous termination of pregnancy. The increasing age of the father also seems to be associated with increased risk for autism. Though they encountered no dramatic factor that by itself led to the syndrome, these researchers nonetheless uncovered a pattern of risks that seem to precede, or at least accompany, the birth of a child with autism. This pattern can be considered as a possible marker for the disorder by counselors and by others who consider the lifestyles and circumstances of families whose children may be at risk for, or who suffer from, the disorder.

In a similar contextually situated manner to the North Dakota study, the work of Michael Rutter and his associates with children adopted from Rumanian orphanages and living in the United Kingdom also considers the social milieu of children with autism. Children from the Rumanian institutions, the researchers found, had developed characteristics similar to autism because of profound deprivation. Another study that similarly examines the sociocultural and physical situation of children with autism points out that autisticlike symptoms also appear in children who are congenitally blind (Brown, Hobson, & Lee, 1997, cited in Rutter, 1999). These studies suggests that even though some behaviors unlike ordinary autism were present in both the deprived and the blind children, particular attention must be paid to the details and circumstances of a child with social and communicative deficits and repetitive behaviors, since it seems clear that there are several ways in which such autisticlike characteristics develop (Rutter, 1999).

Though contextual considerations clearly have some role to play in the appearance of autism symptoms, most of the current research explores the possible genetic causes of the disorder rather than the likely risk factors and familial attributes, though it is necessarily the case that families and their individual members still lie at the heart of these genetic inquiries. We also will begin our discussion with both families and children, for they are the main participants in the story that we have been telling from the very first.

As we saw earlier, autism affects families and children in certain predictable numbers in populations everywhere. We have seen, for example, that studies of autism indicate that the classically defined syndrome is to be found in two to four individuals out of every ten thousand in any population and that boys are three to four times more likely to be affected than are girls. In a more specific manner, however, if we shift our gaze to smaller groups of people, say to just particular families and children, we discover that recent studies of individual families with autistic members have provided even more definite insights into the relationship of numbers to specific individuals and their relatives. These more tightly focused studies have, for example, indicated that 3 percent of families with autism have more than one child with the disorder and the recur-

rence risk for a family of having a second child with the syndrome is 6 to 8 percent, a value one hundred to two hundred times the rate expected by chance
(Folstein, Bisson, Santangelo, & Piven, 1998). Studies of twins present particularly useful perspectives on the inheritance of this disorder, too.
Monozygotic or identical twins appear to have a 36 percent to as high as an 82
percent occurrence of particular artistic traits in both twins when a broader
range of cognitive and social abnormalities is used to mark the disorder.
Dyzygotic or fraternal twins have a zero to 10 percent shared occurrence of autistic traits when using the same broader range of abnormalities to indicate the
syndrome (Trottier, Srivastava, & Walker, 1998). After pooling the data from
such family-based studies, a heritability rate of 91 to 93 percent can be calcu-
lated for autism in families with autistic children (Insel, O'Brien, & Leckman,
1999). These family and twin studies have also allowed for the recognition of a
wider autistic type of individual. This is significant, for not only has such recognition indicated that entire families may frequently exhibit to a greater or lesser
degree traits related to the autistic disorder, but it has also made it possible to
ascertain that autisticlike traits extend far beyond the definition of classical autism, Asperger syndrome, or PDD-NOS (pervasive developmental disorder
not otherwise specified), and present themselves as a broader series of autistic
traits that define a type. This type is distinguished by visible characteristics of
"conceptually similar" cognitive and social behaviors and personality characteristics. These traits include early language-related difficulties, pragmatic language deficits, social reticence, and a tendency to keep to rigid routines
(Folstein, Bisson, Santangelo, & Piven, 1998). The clustering of such similarly
affected individuals in families could, of course, indicate that environmental
factors are significant in the appearance of autism; however, it is also as likely to
be further evidence of a genetic involvement in the disorder (Maestrini, Marlow, Weeks, & Monaco, 1998).

Even though there appears to be a vast array of possibilities for research in
families, really extensive family studies are extremely difficult to undertake in
the search for the link between autism and genes both because of the frequent
presence of the many autisticlike traits in several members of such families and
because of the still uncertain mode of inheritance of the disorder (Folstein, et
al., 1998). There are several additional factors that make such research difficult. First, families faced with the difficulties of raising a child with autism frequently limit their family size to one child; second, because of their social
abnormalities, people with autism rarely have children, thus making it nearly
impossible to study two or more generations at a time. However, DNA, the
basic material in the chromosomes of all living things, when taken from a single
child with autism can be also be used, especially in studies looking for the "can-

didate genes" for autism. Candidate genes are genes for which there is some reason to think they may contribute to the cause of autism (Folstein, et al.).

To tackle the problem of which genes may be at fault in the creation of autism, comparisons of the genetic structure of large, unrelated groups of individuals with the disorder frequently play an important role in research, and since the genes themselves reside in chromosomes (humans have twenty-three pairs of these rodlike forms), it is on these larger structures that much research is focused.

Christopher Gillberg (1998), a Swedish researcher, uses just such large surveys and national registries to uncover a number of people with autism. His findings indicate that, among other things, one chromosome is particularly notable for its frequency of abnormality in the individuals that make up his statistics, and moreover, one specific location on the chromosome's structure is similarly frequently damaged. Based on these findings, Gillberg considers chromosome 15, especially the q-arm or long arm, to be a likely location for the abnormality that leads to the development of autism (p. 419). (An arm is determined relative to the centromere or more condensed area of a chromosome. There is both a long arm or q-arm and a p-arm or short arm on a chromosome, [Hamkalo, 1991]). Gillberg also uncovered evidence that it is possible that the genes that produce autism may be located on chromosomes 5, 8, 17, and 18 (pp. 417–421).

Other investigators, too, have suggested chromosome 15 as a likely site for the aberrations that cause autism, since these investigators likewise have discovered a number of duplications of small parts in the chromosome's long arm in people with the syndrome. For example, Lauritsen, Mors, Mortensen, and Ewald (1999) also point to the significance of chromosome 15, remarking that "[t]he most frequently reported aberration in the literature survey concerns chromosome 15q11–13" (p. 342). The critical nature of 15q11–13 is also evidenced by the fact that it has been found to be the region involved in Prader-Willi syndrome, a condition characterized by obesity, mental retardation, and testicular atrophy or decrease in the production of germinal cells, Angelman syndrome, characterized by jerky movements, protruding tongue, bouts of laughter, lack of speech, retardation, and flat head (*Merritt's Textbook of Neurology*, 1995), and the inv dup(15) syndrome characterized by autism, seizures, and severe mental retardation (Lauritsen, et al.).

Other genes and chromosomes also have been put forward as involved in the development of autism. The serotonin transporter gene (serotonin is a neurotransmitter that regulates mood, among other things), for example, may also be at fault, since certain drugs that affect serotonin can ameliorate some characteristic autistic behaviors. This suggests that "[t]he most likely genes to be candidates for causing autism are those that regulate serotonin biochemistry" (Folstein, et al., 1998 p. 442). An additional association with autism has been found between two markers on the c-harvey ras (HRAS) gene on chromosome 11, since in the fetus this gene is involved in the proliferation and differentiation of neural crest cells, a group of embryonic cells that are derived from the roof of the neural tube and that give rise to a variety of adult cells (*Oxford Dictionary of Biochemistry and Molecular Biology*, 2000). After birth, these neural crest cells take part in sending important messages between cells that instruct still other cells when to grow and divide (Folstein, et al., 1998). Thus, this gene, too, may play a role in producing the physical and neurological abnormalities frequently found in individuals with autism, since the syndrome appears to begin during early fetal development and to cease forever after the changes for the disorder are complete.

Additionally, chromosomes 16 and 17 may be significant in the causes of autism since aberrations on chromosome 16 are the second-most frequently reported abnormalities after those on chromosome 15 (Lauritsen, et al., 1999). Malformations on chromosome 16 have also produced sixty-six cases diagnosed with childhood psychosis and forty-six cases diagnosed with autism, with eight of the cases containing the same fragile site. Chromosome 17 is of apparent interest, too, since four cases have been reported with deletions in the exact same location on this chromosome (Lauritsen, et al., 1999, p. 342).

The only chromosomes that have not yet been implicated in autism or autisticlike behaviors according to Gillberg's (1998) investigations of chromosomal disorders are chromosomes 12, 14, and 20. The remainder, chromosomes 1, 2, 3, 4, 5, 6, 7, 8, 9, 10, 11, 13, 15, 16, 17, 18, 19 (though only one boy with atypical autism/Asperger syndrome was reported for chromosome 19), 21, 22, and the *X* and *Y*, have each been implicated to greater or lesser degrees. This relationship of the *X* sex chromosome to autism can be deduced from the number of autistic behaviors in people with fragile *X* syndrome, an inherited condition found mainly in males and characterized by mental retardation, large ears, long faces, slightly smaller heads, and enlarged testes (Adams, Victor, & Ropper, 1997), even though the majority of such individuals do not have fully developed autism.

Significantly, however, other researchers have not been able to duplicate the studies that indicate the involvement of chromosome 15q11–13 in autism and in fact, have obtained "[s]trong negative results . . . though this region should still be viewed as an area of strong interest, given the number of reports showing association between autism" and abnormalities in this region (Salmon, et al., 1999). At the same time, other researchers have taken an altogether different direction, pointing out that most cases of autism and pervasive development disorders do not show chromosome abnormalities on examination of the genetic material of people affected with these conditions. Additionally, even though fragile *X* syndrome of all the genetic abnormalities shows the strongest link to autism, it appears in only 2 to 16 percent of cases (Ghaziuddin & Burmeister, 1999). Despite such reservations, however, Mohammad Ghaziuddin and Margit Burmeister nonetheless point out that chromosome 15 may have more than a chance association with autism. What is of particular interest for them, however, is not chromosome 15, but chromosome 2, and most specifically, deletion of 2 q37 and its role in a possible subtype of autism marked by distinct physical characteristics (262–263).

These characteristics, found in two boys with autisticlike behaviors and mental retardation, include deep-set eyes with dark circles underneath, depressed nasal bridges, bulging foreheads, and long eyelashes. Such specific repeated attributes may indicate several things: that this is a distinct, though rare, type of autism; that a subgroup of people with autism might be of this type; that the gene in chromosome 2 q37 may be found to be an unexpected or novel one (Ghaziuddin & Burmeister, 1999).

This description of a possible type of autism, though an admittedly infrequently occurring one, illustrates for us the complexity of research into the causes of the syndrome itself. It points out not only the presence of various subgroups of autistic disorders, but also suggests again the likelihood of multiple causes for the syndrome. These include not only the infectious agents, metabolic disorders, and chromosomal abnormalities (Ghaziuddin & Burmeister, 1999) mentioned before, but also in-utero exposure to some type of viral infection, rubella (measles), or to birth defect–causing substances such as ethanol, valproic acid, or thalidomide. Additionally, people with certain genetic diseases such as phenylketonuria, an inborn metabolic disorder of the amino acids that if untreated can cause metal retardation, seizures, and uneven hair pigmentation, and tuberous sclerosis, an inherited disorder that is characterized by mental retardation, skin lesions and tumors of the nervous system and viscera, and seizures (*Merritt's Textbook of Neurology*, 1995), have a greater chance of having autism (Rodier, 2000). At the same time, an immune dysfunction may play a role, as might either prenatal or perinatal brain damage (Frith, 1995).

Another consideration in the genetic underpinning of autism regards the mechanism of inheritance of the disorder, for such a mechanism must also account for the considerable variation in the syndrome's severity and characteristics—characteristics that alter from individual to individual, family to family. These many variations suggest the possibility that at least two to four genes underly autism, though it is not impossible that as many as ten or more genes are involved in this condition. Whatever the number, however, several genes could interact in many different ways to cause the condition. This suggestion that multiple genes might cause autism is not an unusual state of affairs, for diabetes and some types of cardiovascular disease are also the result of several genes working together (Folstein, et al., 1998).

Certainly it is clear that genes may eventually suggest an explanation for the cause of autism, but what does this mean for the individual who carries them? How do the various physical and behavioral characteristics of autism develop from either damage or heredity? And when do such events begin within the body of an individual child?

EMBRYOLOGY AND NEUROBIOLOGY

To address these questions and to expand our understanding of autism and the physiological changes that are its markers, we must return to the individual and consider how genes behave in the earliest months of his/her fetal life. To do this, we will turn again to Rodier, with whom we began this chapter's discussion, for Rodier herself begins not only with the story of her developing research interest, but with the image of a child, a little boy reaching solemnly for an enormous soap bubble that hangs forever suspended just beyond his reach.

During a lecture by pediatric ophthalmologists Marilyn T. Miller and Kerstin Strömland, Rodier was astonished to discover that 5 percent of the thalidomide victims in Strömland's and Miller's research (cited in Rodier, 2000), all Swedish adults born in the late 1950s and early 1960's, have autism, a 30 percent higher rate than is found in the general population (in Rodier, 2000). With her background in embryology, Rodier was especially interested in their results, for the well-known dreadful consequences of early thalidomide exposure become visible in a fetus in a particular manner that indicates the period of development when the drug was present. Though Miller's and Strömland's research was particularly focused on eye motility problems from thalidomide exposure in utero, what especially engaged Rodier, were physical malformations and autism. These physical manifestations include a variety of specific malformations: stunted arms and legs, misshaped or missing ears and thumbs, and neurological damage to eye and face muscles. As an embryologist Rodier was able to see this wide array of physical defects as an indication of the time the damage itself occurred, as a literal physical time line of thalidomide's destructive influence on a developing fetus. "The thumb" for example, "is affected as early as twenty-two days after conception, the ears from days twenty to thirty-three, and the arms and legs from days twenty-five to thirty-five" (Rodier, 2000, p. 59). Most importantly, however, these malformations suggested the possibility that they could pinpoint the period of time in which autism itself began. Rodier's growing excitement at the relationship of autism, certain physical malformations, and the stage of fetal development was finally fanned into flame by Miller and Strömland's additional discovery that "Most of the thalidomide victims with autism had anomalies in the external part of their ears but no malformations of the arms and legs," suggesting that "the subjects had been injured very early in gestation—twenty to twenty-four days after conception—before many women know they are pregnant" (p. 59). Discovering *when* something occurs tells an embryologist *what,* and *what* provides the key to understanding accidental changes during fetal development and for Rodier, perhaps the source of the characteristics of autism itself.

During the fourth week of gestation few neurons or nerve cells form, and most are motor neurons of the cranial nerves that operate the muscles of the eyes, throat, ears, face, jaws, and tongue. These motor neurons are in the brain stem, the area between the spinal cord and brain. Because these neurons are developing at the same time as the external ears, Rodier suggests that it is possible to predict that people who have been affected by thalidomide will also suffer from dysfunctions of their cranial nerves. This is so, according to Miller and Strömland. Such individuals with autism have abnormalities of facial expressions and eye movements; and sometimes both are affected (Rodier, 2000).

However, the appearance of children with autism is not necessarily one of malformation and misaligned body parts. As Rodier hastens to point out, not only do children with autism often look physically normal, but they are, in fact, frequently exceptionally beautiful, a fact that others have noticed, too. Park (1982), for example, describes her two-year-old daughter Jessy this way: "A bronzed, gold baby of unusual beauty . . . many people look at her because she is so pretty," (p. 5). A friend of the Parks called Jessy "a fairy child" moved by her golden hair, blue eyes, and "the dancing grace of her body" (p. 5). Children with autism like Jessy often are not only lovely, but also of normal height and weight.

However, children with autism frequently lack facial expressions, have abnormal eye movements, and have mouths with corners lower than the middle portion of the upper lip (Rodier, 2000). Park writes also of facial expressions, of Jessy's curious lack of response to other people as an eighteen-month-old and of her expressiveness only in a private, personal way: "She does not look up though she is smiling and laughing; she does not call our attention to the mysterious object of her pleasure. She does not see us at all. She and the spot are all there is" (p. 3). Additionally, among the other, minor physical changes that have been noted in autism, the ears of children with the syndrome catch Rodier's attention because of both their unusual appearance and what they seem to indicate about the genesis of the disorder. Children with autism, she writes, more often than other children have low-set, square-shaped ears that bend forward at the top. The ear itself is often tilted to the rear more than 15 degrees. So it is ears, their early formation in the development of a fetus, and their unusual characteristics in people with autism that bring Rodier and us, too, back to the possible moment of autism's genesis, to the twenty to twenty-fourth day of gestation and the development of the brain itself.

At the same time the external ear is developing in a fetus, the nervous system and brain are beginning to form. The brain stem begins to develop, too, as the cell bodies that operate the ears, face, tongue, jaw, and throat, motor neurons of the cranial nerves, begin to grow in the region between the brain and the spinal cord. Since Miller's and Strömland's (in Rodier, 2000, pp. 56–63) subjects with autism had abnormalities of eye movement or facial expression or both—conditions often found in a person with autism—it suggests that it is during this time of brain stem development that the changes of autism begin.

The brain stem, the portion of the central nervous system that formed the focal point of the thalidomide study, had not been of particular concern in the early search for the causes of autism since it had been considered as merely the seat of basic functions—breathing, eating, sleeping, coordination, balance, and so on (Rodier, 2000). Additionally, many of the disturbances of autism had been believed to be controlled by higher portions of the brain, including the cerebral cortex, a sheet of neurons that covers the surface of the cerebral hemispheres and plays a role in language, abstract thinking, and basic aspects of movement and other responses (Nolte, 1999), and the hippocampus, a major component of the limbic system that plays a critical role in the formation of new memories (Nolte & Angevine, 1995). However, some of the symptoms of autism—lack of facial expressions, hypersensitivity to sight, sound, touch, and taste that are problematic for people with this disorder and the sleep disturbances that may be a part of the syndrome for many people—have to do with the portion of the brain that deals with basic functions. Significantly, in the increasing number of postmortem exams of people with autism the most frequently reported abnormality in their brains is not a change in the forebrain but in the reduction of the number of neurons in the cerebellum, "[a] large processing center of the hindbrain that has been know to have critical functions in the control of muscle movement" (p. 61). Additionally, several of the brains examined in such studies were found to be of a particularly large size, and abnormalities were found in both the brain stem and in the cortex. At the same time, as Kanner first mentioned, the heads of some people with autism are larger, too (Rutter, 1999).

Further indication of enlarged brains in at least some people with autism can be found in the MRI (magnetic resonance imaging) scans of the brains of twenty-two high-functioning males that demonstrated in 40 percent of those examined an increased brain size (Piven, et al., 1995). In theory, there are three possible reasons for brain enlargement in individuals with autism that are the result of developmental processes in the brain. First, more neurons may have been created initially; second, fewer nerve cells may have died off during normal developmental processes; third, more brain tissue and blood vessels may have been created. In order to determine which of these three hypotheses explains the development of substantially larger brain sizes in some individuals with autism, additional studies must be undertaken. Such examinations must explore the following issues: First, sufficient neuropathological examinations must be performed to verify the actual structures of the brain. Second, females with autism must be included in imaging research as well as people with other neurological disorders. And third, subregions of the brain must be examined to decide whether the brain's enlargement is caused by increased overall brain size or the increased size of only a particular portion of the organ. Additionally, it must be discovered whether autistic people with enlarged brains form a sub-group within the disorder of autism or whether enlarged brains have a more general role in the syndrome in an as yet undisclosed manner (Piven, et al., 1995). An additional related point of particular interest is the recent revelation made by psychiatrist Nancy Andreasen, director of the University of Iowa Mental Health Clinic Research Center and one of the researchers in the study with Piven et al. Though her research is not directly connected with autism it-self, it nonetheless provides an example of one possible mechanism for the de-velopment of brain abnormalities during the human maturation process. Andreasen, who is particularly interested in uncovering the biomolecular mechanisms that underlie schizophrenia, finds, "People with schizophrenia are impaired in different cognitive ways such as memory, attention, and lan-guage. Yet neuroimaging studies reveal dysfunction within the cortical re-gions, cerebellum, and thalamus no matter what function is involved" (Researcher unravels, 2000, p. 11). She explains further that the brain com-pletes its wiring between the ages of fifteen and thirty by pruning, shaping, and sculpting its axons, the part of the nerve cell through which impulses are car-ried away from the cell body and dendrites, the branched portion of a nerve cell that carries impulses toward the cell body to ensure that the nerves are con-nected properly. In schizophrenia, however, something seems to go wrong with this process because of "aberrant molecular regulation" (p. 11). Perhaps similar failures of developmental processes underlie the enlarged brains of at least some people with autism, as suggested earlier (Piven, et al., 1995, pp. 1147–1148).

At the very least, such findings indicate that a single small brain lesion could not be the cause of autism. Nonetheless, it is hard to know just how im-portant these findings might be, though such results might indicate the age when the developmental process began to go wrong, or that the brain was in-volved in a systemwide malfunction (Rutter, 1999). Grandin herself asserts that autism is a neurological disorder that can be found in the makeup of the brain during a variety of examinations. Bauman's and Kemper's study (cited in Grandin, 1995a) found that different subtypes of autism have a similar pattern of immature development of the cerebellum and the limbic system. The limbic system plays an important part in memory, emotional responses, and related behaviors (Nolte, 1999). However, "There may be slight variations in the pattern which could account for more severe sensory-processing problems at the regressive end of the spectrum," and hence more trouble with concreteness of thinking at the other end (Grandin, 1995a, p. 141). Grandin points out that cerebellar abnormalities could also account for sensory oversensitivity and that brain stem abnormalities might be able to explain the sensory jumbling and mixing she so graphically describes. MRI scans of her own brain, Grandin explains, indicate that her cerebellum is 20 percent smaller than normal. She attributes her immense mental tenacity on the one hand and her mental inflexibility on the other to these cerebellar abnormalities, though as Sacks (1995) points out, scientific opinion is divided on the likelihood of such a possibility. Another indication of cerebellar involvement in Grandin's autism is her gait, which to Sacks seemed "slightly clumsy or uncouth," as is often the case for adults with autism. Grandin herself, according to Sacks, attributes this to simple "Ataxia [jerky, awkward, poorly controlled body movements] associated with impaired development of the vestibular system and part of the cerebellum." However, though Sacks performed a brief neurological exam focusing on her cerebellar function and balance and though he did find a little ataxia, it was insufficient to explain Grandin's unusual awkwardness (Sacks, 1995, p. 256).

Other research from a number of sources includes information that suggests that the brain, its form, and its functions will eventually provide multiple insights into the causes of autism. For example, autistic people with lower IQs tend to have smaller, less developed brain stems, according to some research (Hashimoto, et al. in Grandin, 1995a), and electrical transmission through such brain stems is slower than in higher-function individuals (Grandin, 1995a). Still other research has indicated that individuals with autism have abnormalities of the cerebellar vermis, the midline zone of the cerebellum, the Purkinje cells, sole output neurons from the cerebellar cortex, and the granular cells, axons in the cerebellum that lead to the deeper cerebellar nuclei layers (Nolte & Angevine, 1995), in addition to changes in the relative cell size and density of the hippocampus. Additionally, PET (photon emission tomography) and SPECT (single photon emission computed tomography) examinations have indicated that perhaps the frontal and/or temporal regions of the brain may be the source of the disorder (Potgieter & Fryns, 1999).

Neurotransmitters, those biochemical substances stored in the axon of a neuron that transmit impulses to another neuron, muscle cell, or other excitable cell or that inhibit such transmission have been suspected as playing a role in autism for some time. In 1978 it was proposed that the neurotransmitter dopamine, which projects mainly into basal ganglia but also into parts of the frontal and temporal lobes, was a possible culprit in causing autism. The temporal lobes have four main functions, according to Nolte and Angevine: (1) as primary auditory cortex; (2) in comprehension of language; (3) in higher-order processing of visual information; and (4) as involved in complex aspects of learning and memory. Though the hypothesis was based on the similarities among lesioned laboratory animals, schizophrenic patients, and children with autism, the correspondence between the symptoms of autism, including "strange gait, poor voice control, apparently expressionless faces, flapping hand movements, repetitious actions, lack of spontaneity, perseveration on one topic, and social impairments" are suggestive of just such a dysfunction of the dopamine system (Damasio & Maurer in Frith, 1995, pp. 75–76). At the same time, catecholaminergic neurotransmitters, norepinephrine, dopamine, and epinephrine, chemical transmitters found in the body that together regulate mood, stress, fear, anger, attention, movement, behavior, and the release of hormones from the pituitary gland, may also play a role, since elevated levels of these substances have been found in the blood and urine of people with autism. More recently, however, attention has focused on the role of oxytocin and vasopressin, peptides synthesized in the hypothalamus, released into the bloodstream and traditionally considered endocrine hormones that act on peripheral organs. However, these substances have been reexamined and are now considered "[n]eurotransmitters or neuromodulators, that is, peptides with central action" (Insel, O'Brien, & Leckman, 1999). In nonhumans these neuropeptides influence behaviors that are characteristic of autism, including deficits in communication, social, and cognitive behaviors, and various stereotyped behaviors. More specifically, in animal studies these substances have been found to affect learning and memory, particularly "social memory," which includes the recognition of cohorts, learning factors about the mother (at least in rat pups), maternal behavior, social attachments, pair-bonding, nest defense as well as other sociosexual behaviors, aggression, and self-injurious behaviors (Insel, et al., 1999). Several studies of neuropeptides in human subjects, though not related to autism, also suggest the possibility that these neurotransmitters may have a role in the autism syndrome.

Most remarkable among these studies, however, is the point of view of the relationship of these neuropeptides to human behavior. Postmortem examinations of depressed subjects found a significant increase in both vasopressin (56 percent) and oxytocin (23 percent) positive cells in the hypothalamus, and an inquiry found that obsessive-compulsive patients without tics may have increased oxytocin concentrations in their cerebrospinal fluid (Insel, et al., 1999). Nonetheless, though such information is not yet available in regard to autism, another recent investigation did indicate that the plasma concentration of oxytocin in autistic children was about half that observed in children without autism and that autistic children did not show the normal developmental increase of plasma oxytocin with either age or interpersonal skills, thus displaying a state of affairs that is "consistent with a genetic deficiency of oxytocin" (Insel, et al., 1999, p. 152). Another suggestion that these neuropeptides might have a role in autism comes from a study in which the administration of oxytocin to autistic children was reported to increase their sociability (Hollander, in Insel, et al., 1999). It seems reasonable, therefore, to conclude from these various studies that vasopressin and oxytocin neural pathways in both animals and humans have at least species-appropriate effects on social behaviors, communication, cognition, and stereotyped or repetitive behaviors. Thus, it is not too farfetched to consider the possibility that these systems have a role in autism since these are the very behaviors that are affected in the syndrome (Insel, et al., 1999).

An altogether different research direction unrelated to work with neurotransmitters was pursued by Rodier and her research team, for while they were pursuing the connection between thalidomide, embryology, and autism in 1995, they had the chance to examine the brain of a woman with autism who had died in the 1970s. What they discovered was revealing, for not only were there marked changes in the form of the brain stem itself, there were significant changes at the cellular level, too. Perhaps the most marked alterations, however, were the reduction in size of the facial nucleus, which controls the muscles that cause facial expressions, and the absence of the superior olive, a brain structure that relays auditory information. Additionally, a count of the facial neurons "showed only about four hundred cells, whereas counts of the facial neurons in a control brain showed nine thousand" (Rodier, 2000, p. 61). Significantly, these malformed or missing organs arise from the same section of the embryonic structure that eventually develops into the central nervous system—the neural tube. Another unusual characteristic of the woman's brain was that though it was slightly heavier than average, a portion of the brain stem seemed to be missing altogether. As Rodier explains, "It was as though a band of tissue had been cut out of the brain stem, and the two remaining pieces had been knit back together with no seam where the tissue was missing" (p. 61).

Further examinations and study by the researchers entailed comparing the woman's brain with the brains of transgenic "knockout" mice. (These are mice genetically altered to provide researchers particular gene structures and related physical characteristics; in this case they were engineered to "lack the expression of the gene known as Hoxa1" [p. 61]. The rodents had been created particularly to enable researchers to study that gene's role in early fetal development.) The comparison revealed startling similarities including: shortened brain stems, missing superior olive, and smaller than average facial nucleus. The mice also had additional autismlike physical changes such as ear malformations and a missing brain structure that controls eye movement. Significantly, the knockout gene, Hoxa1, is found on chromosome 7, and though it is inactive after the early stages of neuron development, it plays a central role in the growth of the brain stem itself when the first neurons are forming. At the same time, it is during this critical period in fetal development that thalidomide is thought to cause the disorder of autism. Disappointingly, the mystery surrounding autism was not to be resolved, however, for though Rodier discovered that the single variant of the Hoxa1 gene she was studying was present at a higher rate (40 percent) in people with autism than in their family members or unrelated individuals, it was also present in 20 percent of the people without autism, thus indicating that other genetic factors must also be present to cause the syndrome. (See also Ingram, et al., 2000.)

Once again, in Rodier's studies as in the inquiries of the other researchers we have considered, interesting possibilities for answers to the many questions that surround autism have been uncovered and new directions for research have been suggested. However, no single tangible fact or any solid answers have yet appeared. Nonetheless, we are left with a clearer understanding of the most likely scenarios for the development of the syndrome. First, the neurobiological events that cause autism likely begin early in the development of the central nervous system. Second, they probably involve a "cascade of complex gene-environmental interactions" (Insel, et al., 1999, p. 145). Third, they are "often complicated by neurological, cytogenetic, neurotransmitter, and immunological abnormalities" (Hollander, et al., 1999, p. 1). Taking these possibilities together, we may imagine that not only do the cascading events that cause changes in the early developing fetus likely produce the condition of autism but also that after these events occur, they cease forever along with the completion of the developmental sequence, since autism seems not to be a progressive disorder (Rodier, 2000).

At the same time that research into the causes of autism has increased in quantity and visibility, however, so, too, have the inquiries into the cognitive and neurological characteristics of people with the disorder, both for what these characteristics might suggest about the etiology and nature of the condition and also for what they might indicate regarding possible effective treatment for people who have the syndrome.

The young artists with autism that we have met—Jamie, Katie, Peter, and Mark—will again help us to explore the research that investigates not only the qualities of autism and what these characteristics may indicate about the disorder itself, but also how these same qualities may be discovered to play a role in the precocious art making of these children. As we discovered early on, the characteristics of art made by children with autism frequently include a shared graphic style as well as a recognizable series of preoccupations and a quality of fierce specificity that catches the eye with its vigorous rendering of a particular subject. Jamie and his masterful architectural and auto drawings, Katie and her cavorting, expressive animals, Mark and his hurling rockets, and Peter and his engaging, always lively Disney-esque characters come to mind for the particular quality of "thisness," of the intense individual, momentary glimpse of the subject at hand in their art. Sacks (1985, 1995) first pointed out this visual quality of an arrested moment and vigorous individual presence in the drawings of José, one of his earlier patients, and later in the architectural images of Stephen Wiltshire, remarking on both individuals' vigorous use of line and uncanny ability to describe objects.

This sense of the presence of things, of a swift rendering of the momentary, the individual, and the particular that can be discovered in the art of the artists with autism we have seen can likely be understood to reflect in large measure the characteristics of the preattentive aspects of the vision process itself with its bias toward rapid computation, description of outline and surface, and accurate assessment of three-dimensional form and spatial location. Certainly, such attributes indicate a literal visual source for such vigorous linear-rendering abilities. In addition, our further surmise of such young artists' unbiased encounter with the visual world free from sociocultural constraints also likely plays a role. Clearly, however, this is not the entire story, for visual memory is also an obvious ingredient here, and an awesome level of visual acuity appears to operate based on the briefest, most sidelong of glances. Something in the young artists' attention and looking itself needs to be explained.

The struggle in drawing for any artist is not the creation of a generalized view, but rendering the nature of particular things, describing the visual characteristics that make articles most themselves and unlike any other object of their type that might be similar to them. The art of caricature, for example, depends for its punch on these same particularizing qualities pushed to an extreme—a large nose swells to an enormous, lumpy affair, small eyes become mere dots or disappear altogether, bushy eyebrows sprout into vast thickets of tangled lines. These exaggerations not only assist the viewer in easily identifying the subject, but also enable him or her to grasp the essence of the subject's actual physical presence and demeanor.

Unlike a caricaturist, however, young children without autism as they first begin to draw employ generalized qualities and cultural conventions to express concepts of things in schema—a tree may consist of two parallel lines with a bulgy, misshaped ball for leaves, a flower may display teardrop-shaped petals or a half ellipse with a saw-toothed edge, a house may be formed from an assembly of rectangles, triangles, and squares elaborated with a doorknob, spiraling smoke, and curtains that resemble the rear leg of a quadruped in form. Adults who are not artists also produce similar generalized views of things, creating images that stand for entire categories, basic forms that relate information through the use of common features. It is this generalized quality of their images that causes most nonartists, child and adult alike, to throw down their drawing pencil in disgust and claim they cannot draw.

As we discovered earlier, the attention of children with autism seems to be seized by peculiar objects—by floating fat and ventilator grates, by toys in files and electrical outlets, and by the minutia of mirror mounts and two-pronged plugs. How might one account for such preoccupations, and what might they have to do with a sense of immediacy and skill in art, and what are the results of such focused attention to other aspects of their lives? The obsessive attention to specific stimuli in their environment by people with autism, a consistently baffling behavior in this disorder, has frequently been held responsible for their failure to transfer newly acquired skills from one environment to another, since their overselectivity interferes with their ability to generalize learning (Plaisted, O'Riordan, & Baron-Cohen, 1998a). However, this may not necessarily be the case. A recent study advanced the hypothesis that individuals with autism process unique features extremely well and common features poorly in comparison to nonautistic individuals. This in turn suggests an altogether different perspective on obsessive attention and failure to generalize behaviors. The hypothesis was borne out, for in an examination of high-functioning adults with autism, results suggested that, "individuals with autism are better able than non-autistic individuals to solve novel discrimination problems involving highly similar stimuli" (p. 772). At the same time, as had been predicted, people with the syndrome did poorly on generalization tasks in relationship to people without the disorder since "generalization depends on the extent to which a subject processes or recognizes common features" (p. 773). In the end, however, a new perspective is suggested on this disorder, one that casts such differences in a different light, for "[a]lthough autism is usually characterized as a disability, it is also clear that . . . autism can be characterized as an unusual pattern of strengths" (p. 774). A companion study done at the same time also indicates that people with autism have significant related abilities—"superior visuospacial skills" and the ability to detect objects of interest (Plaisted, O'Riordan, & Baron-Cohen, 1998b, p. 782).

Such results suggest not only other sources for the remarkably keen eyes and clear memories of artists with autism besides the visual system itself, but also additional sources for the accuracy and energy that suffuse the images of many artists with autism, sources that are evident in the skills that are put to use in the uncanny caricatures of Jonathan as well as the astonishingly detailed, specific architectural drawings of Stephen and Jamie. As we have seen, the artist's eye is most often on the specific, the individual, the novel, not on the features that are common to all. But what about the shared, the generalized, the similar? Do these findings have some insights into the creation of images of common features, too? The answer here is perhaps yes, for such a disability may partially explain the rather surprisingly frequent lack of skill of some precocious young artists to draw people well; Peter, Jamie, Mark, and even Katie draw the human figure using cursory, generalized schematic forms, though clearly Jonathan provides an exception, which we will address later.

Another perspective on these same knotty problems of vision, memory, art, and autism can be found in the implications that arise from the recent examinations of the modular nature of the vision process itself. As we saw earlier, for example, brain damage can selectively affect the ability to see objects presented in different perspectives (Marr, 1982). One can see but not be aware of doing so (Cowey, 1995), and it is possible for a person with right hemisphere damage to see the whole of something but not all of its parts (Marshall & Halligan, 1995). Similarly, the visual memory system itself is divided into independent systems that are also each separately susceptible to damage. What is especially significant for us, however, is that recent studies with individuals with autism suggest that their visual memory systems may be selectively damaged in utero (Cipolotti, Robinson, Blair, & Frith, 1999). Thus, it is possibly because of such damage that people with autism may fail to develop recognition memory of unfamiliar faces of both humans and animals. It has been demonstrated that such recognition is separate from the development of visual topographical memory—visual memory of unknown buildings, scenes, and landmarks (Cipolotti, et al., 1999). Though the question remains as to the relationship of this impairment of memory for unknown faces and animals to autism, it nonetheless suggests fertile ground for further research. For our purposes, however, it is the topographic memory of landmarks, scenes, and buildings that concerns us most here, for such memory likely plays an important role in the creation of particular images in the art of precocious artists with autism. Evidence for this can be found in the work of several of the artists we have seen.

If we return to the creations of these artists, we find that buildings, specific rooms, and particular qualities of landscapes and spaces are not uncommon subjects. Stephen, Jamie, and Jessy all are entranced by the specifics of built space and architectural complexity. Jamie recalls each change in the surface of a wall, each door and window, every turn of a spiral stair, describing with ease the sweep of a room and the objects in it. Stephen draws entire facades and interiors of elaborate architectural monuments with professional flair, creating vigorous images dense with the details of even the most subtle ornaments. Jessy, in turn, paints only the exterior view of buildings, breaking their surfaces into blocks of color that describe and highlight every change of texture and depth, and distinguish details. Mark, though not in the least interested in buildings, nonetheless concentrates on the details and architectonic forms of rockets, nonliving, spatial constructions, objects that are not unlike buildings in their interior structures and exterior, geometric forms.

Katie and Peter, unlike these other artists, explore the world of fantasy with nonhuman characters. These characters are, however, held safely at a distance by the plastic world of videotape and cartoon conventions. True, these are not landmarks, scenes, or architecture in the usual sense, but to an observer who absorbs hours of repeated viewings, these images may have a similar effect, for visually they register as nonliving, constructed, spatially located objects in carefully described scenes and settings: things—objects, really—not living animals or people. Even Dorothy and the Wizard, who are certainly human in the original *Wizard of Oz*, have become cartoon figures in Peter's drawings. At the same time, they play a smaller role than other characters in his images. The other, distinctly nonhuman characters present a smaller drawing challenge, for most of them are already costumed in such a way as to turn them into something other than living creatures.

Of all the artists we have seen, however, only Jonathan tackles drawing living human faces, though it is important to understand that he does so in a manner that treats them like building facades—distorted, exaggerated, almost satirical—rendering them as constructions, collections of shapes, and not at all portraits of real people in the usual sense of portraiture and realistic imagery. Even though Jonathan is our only example of an artist with autism with any interest in drawing the human face, he is nonetheless stylistically allied with the creators of more topographic images at the same time, as a cartoonist and explorer of surface and line. Perhaps he is able to remember the faces of strangers so clearly because they are reduced to a collection of disembodied shapes and nonhuman visual elements.

In addition to questions of memory deficits for certain objects and perhaps unknown faces above all, there are indications that something is amiss in the attention that children with autism pay to people and other social stimuli even from the earliest months of life (Swettenham, et al., 1998). Using three groups of twenty-month-old infants, one with autism, one developmentally delayed, and one of typically developing infants, the researchers observed the "spontaneous distribution and patterning of attention in terms of looking behavior" in all three groups (p. 751). These findings revealed that even young infants with autism spent less time looking at people than did infants in the other two groups. Additionally, the infants with autism spent more time looking at objects than did the other children, and they switched their attention less frequently between social and nonsocial stimuli. Such behaviors indicate that social abnormalities are present at an early age and have serious implications for delays in the development of many kinds of social abilities later on (Swettenham, et al., 1998).

However, even these findings might have positive qualities for precocious young artists with autism, for they suggest an increased ability for looking at the world of objects and things in a more sustained manner than many other children and young adults their own age. Since seeing is the basis of engagement with the visual world, and looking closely at what one wishes to draw or paint is one of the first and most important skills developed by any artist, this absorption with a visual world of nonhuman objects might provide a boon for budding architects/artists like Jamie and Stephen, landscape painters like Richard, space rocket designers like Mark, or cartoonists like Katie and Peter.

More time looking at objects, better memory for buildings, scenes, and landmarks, excellent ability to process unique visual features—all these indications of an autistic person's particular engagement with the visual world suggest the possible sources of some of the preoccupations and strengths that artists with autism brings to their art. Surely, as suggested in regard to the ability to select and process unique features well (Plaisted, et al., 1998a,b), these other characteristics, in addition to a keen eye for uncommon features, can also perhaps be seen as patterns of unusual strengths, at least for an artist with the disorder.

The ability to describe the intense "thisness" of the visual world mentioned first by Sacks (1995) and encountered by us later in the children we met can perhaps be partially explained by these attributes of attention and orientation as well as the characteristics and functions of the vision process itself. Such an explanation certainly would shed additional light on the remarkable graphic abilities that young artists with autism bring to their art.

TOPOGRAPHY AND THE SHAPE OF EXPERIENCE

It was a warm spring morning and the school year was drawing to a close. I fell into conversation at the end of class with a graduate student and former art teacher, considering in a desultory manner some of the things a teacher learns about young art makers from firsthand classroom experience. Since she knew I had a particular interest in the subject of young artists with autism and because of her own amazement at his unusual skills and preoccupations, she shared her memories of a young boy in one of her art classes some years ago. She explained, "He almost always drew himself at the dining room table eating breakfast. It was usually a bird's-eye view, too, one that looked down on the top of his head, his meal, and every piece of furniture in the room." Though the boy's hovering view, his special interest in breakfast, his consideration of the specifics of the dining room, and his solitary meal were his most frequent subjects, she also described his other art interests, briefly remarking, "Of course, he drew architecture, too. He was a sweet little guy." We moved on to other topics, but the boy stayed in my mind as both an idiosyncratic young artist in his own right and as a child closely related to other precocious young artists with autism in many stylistic and content-related ways.

Months later, I recalled the boy and his repeated, unusual three-dimensional drawings of an ordinary daily event, for he seems an exemplar of both the limitations and great strengths to be found in the art of many artists with autism, and he forms a link between the world of research and the other young artists. These several shared connecting links or qualities include the following abilities and disabilities, all attributes evidenced in the boy's art: The first is the boy's adherence to a single topic with infrequent examinations of other subjects, a frequent trait in the art of precocious young artists with autism. The second is his remarkable ability to create, and moreover, to concentrate on drawing three-dimensional architectural space, a recognizable quality of the art of other precocious artists. The third, the boy's exploration of a bird's-eye view that allows for the observation of an entire room at once, ties his art to Jamie's creations particularly, for he, like Jamie, explores a familiar lived family interior from a raised elevation. At the same time the boy's drawings appear to entail topographic memory connecting him to the recent research we have encountered, for his drawings of the family dining room are a simultaneous examination of a portion of a building and a scene, two aspects of such memory that are particularly discovered in the creations of many artists with autism. Clearly, too, he has spent a longer, more significant time visually exploring the familiar familial space, concentrating on its furniture and other fittings to be able to repeat its layout so vigorously in his drawings. Certainly it was not the family members who inhabit the house with him that absorbed his interest, for they never appeared in his breakfast scenes. His eyes were on the objects in the dining space—the table and chair, bowl, spoon, and glass, and the furniture that completes the visual inventory of that specific place.

This greater, more intense involvement with the nonliving world, this eye for architecture and objects, may partially explain both the boy's graphic abilities as he draws himself eating breakfast before school as if he were hovering over the dining room like da Vinci over the Arno, and the skills of the other young artists with autism we have met. They all have the idiosyncratic eye and selective memory that seem to result from the syndrome of autism itself in addition to their own personal preoccupations with creating images from their lives and experiences in a clear-cut, graphic manner.

Using what might be considered in other circumstances a series of weaknesses as an aspect of their skills (Plaisted, et al., 1998a, b), these young artists report their engagement with the world in solid, three-dimensional linear images.

These visual abilities and preoccupations, though perhaps causing difficulty in social settings, may be understood to also enable them to utilize their graphic skills in the development of, and appreciation for, particular content, especially alternative worlds of space and place that form a significant element in many of their drawings. It is this element of world building that forms a bridge between the impersonal character of research and clinical observations and the individual young artists with autism in whom our interest especially lies.

Sacks (1995) points out the importance of fantasy worlds to some individuals with autism in a brief footnote. Though not a clinical tale of autism and its causes, this predilection for alternate worlds is frequently encountered in many high-functioning people with autism, he says. Sacks explains that such high-functioning individuals with autism "describe a great fondness for, almost an addiction to, alternative worlds, imaginary worlds such as those of C. S. Lewis and Tolkien, or worlds they imagine themselves." Illustrating such world-building activities by an entire family (two parents and their son), all of whom have autism, Sacks remarks, "They have spent years constructing an imaginary world with its own landscapes and geography (endlessly mapped and drawn), its own languages, currency, laws, and customs—a world in which fantasy and rigidity play equal parts" (p. 276). This creative activity is of particular interest, for many of the children we have met have individual fantasies in alternative worlds that play major roles in their lives and activities. Although we have looked at their creations and graphic representations and remarked on their narrative, meaning-making qualities, we have not considered their art from the point of view that Sacks's suggestion provides.

The children with whom we have become most familiar—Jamie, Peter, Katie, and Mark—will provide us with the necessary place to begin.

Jamie, known to his classmates as both an artist and writer of some note, creates his own fantasy worlds in ongoing tales of school chaos and disrespect, imaginary people who carry on their lives in one of Jamie's carefully designed houses, or continuous stories of bad boys, auto chases, and jail time in vehicular penitentiaries. Jamie has additional fantasy worlds taken from outside sources, too, places that mirror his personally invented ones in many ways. They, too, highlight disasters, car chase extravaganzas, or battles between crooks and police set in labyrinthian architectural spaces.

"BOOK OF DRAWIN GS dy [sic] Jamie," his newsprint and crayon book, brings together two of these sources of adventure, for it is dedicated to architects at the same time it relates the visual narrative of one of his favorite movies in image upon image of uninhabited, unfurnished, decrepit rooms. In these drawings, it seems, Jamie creates images that bring, to his mind at least, the important moments of the film, for as he turns the pages he relates without a pause the action that takes place in each of these stage set–like crayon images.

Thus, Jamie's alternate world can be seen to be a rich amalgam of imagined events, Hollywood action, local architectural space, and highly detailed illustrations of moments of tension. At least for Jamie, the boundaries between one thing and another seem not so clear, and it is in his drawings and short stories that he finally documents these narratives in a concrete manner.

Peter, also enamored of movies of violence and disaster (though his taste runs to chain saw–wielding maniacs rising from premature burials), is apt to couch his interest in alternate worlds in the language provided by Hollywood films, particularly Disney's fairy tales, or in the several productions of *The Wizard of Oz*. Recently, he has become interested in children's stories (especially those by J.R.R. Tolkien), since both his teacher and the librarian at the small nearby community library encourage him to read and provide him with a variety of classic children's books. As an artist, Peter is most eager to illustrate the adventures from these outside sources rather than invent his own alternative worlds. Because of this, almost his entire artistic output consists of images from these stories, from opening film credits, and especially from moments of greatest peril, as the hero faces almost certain defeat at the hands of the evildoer. The closest Peter has come to the invention of a fantasy world of his own is his book "My Dog Ate Lightening Bugs," a carefully done text and bright marker production that tells the story of a little boy whose dog eats fireflies and then begins to fly himself. On the last page, an image of the moon and three immense four-pointed stars takes up two-thirds of the page. Below, the little boy and his dog return home after a night flying over the globe. The text describes the image. It reads, "My dog flew me back home! He just wanted to eated [sic] some dog food and go to sleep!" This seems a rather cool and impersonal ending to what surely must have been a wild night of adventure. Told in a recognizable children's book style, with an unusual (for Peter) air of meeting adult expectations for children's books and drawings, the creation resembles Peter's other more personal art in its solid bright marker colors and heavy black outlines, though the energy of his other drawings seems to be missing and the story itself seems curiously restrained, unlike his usual more vigorous art.

Katie, like Peter, is most absorbed by the fantasy world she finds in cartoons and Disney productions, for the Berenstain Bears and an array of other animals consisting mainly of rodents form a significant portion of her art's content. Her interest lies in the ordinary homey lives of these animals—in school, at bedtime, during meals—as well as in more slapstick interactions and sounds that are part of the silliness—loud music, the racket of jackhammers, the hum of appliances. Even though no particular continuous narrative ties one image to the next, a familiar fantasy world certainly is present, for each drawing depicts a specific scene, a slice of time, taken from the middle of the hustle and bustle of many animals' lives. Katie's interest in this alternative world of cartoon extremes, this imaginary place where animals have experiences very like humans do, surely can be described as at least a fondness for a universe compounded of cartoons and her own graphic contributions, a special involvement in the goofy world of talking bears and dancing squirrels.

Mark, *Star Trek* devotee, creator of rockets and other-world battles, maker of software containers, and sound man extraordinaire, is the most obvious example of nearly uninterrupted world making comfortably situated within the structure of his similarly engaged family. Not only is Mark's room a place of display for rockets of paper and plastic, but it also mirrors a similar arrangement of shelves displaying rocket models and battle figures that belongs to his parents. For Mark's parents, too, are absorbed in a universe compounded of Dungeons and Dragons and other battle games that they play with friends who are similarly engrossed. Additionally, both parents paint and construct models—especially rockets (his mother) and battle figures (his father) representing characters from favorite games. Mark's is a world compounded of family interests in space adventures, model building, and alternative worlds, space and rocket-related video games, and his own fascination with violent space battles, carefully described rockets, space vehicles, and his father's work at NASA. Mark, like the son of the family described by Sacks, shares this imaginary world with his parents, and all three of them engage in the rich complexity that it contains.

Grandin (1995b) herself can, with a somewhat less literal interpretation of alternative worlds, also be seen to have, even at her most carefully reasoned, some connection here, for her great concentration on, and affection for cattle, her intense commitment to humane slaughter, her belief in God and life after death, all culminate in her humane slaughter system, the "Stairway to Heaven," the outcome of both her creative engineering and visual thinking skills. Surely such a mixture of intuitive and creative abilities, religious belief, and mingled concrete expression and philosophical understanding bears some relationship to the all-absorbing appreciation of a personally imagined alternative world, which, in this case, has a slaughterhouse ramp leading directly to God.

Perhaps a more clear-cut example, however, is that of a middle-aged man with autism, who, when he was younger, drew numerous maps and plans of imaginary college campuses and towns. Certainly these creations serve as examples of alternative worlds, for they were complete with buildings, landmarks, and streets, as well as the details of topography of places that both absorbed his interest at the same time that it exhibited his engagement with both "fantasy and rigidity" (Sacks, 1995).

Though Sacks's (1995) description of many high-functioning autistic people's "fondness for, almost an addiction to, alternate worlds," may be most clearly illustrated by Mark's and his parent's absorption in various imaginary universes, it is also possible to see this same "fondness" in the creations of other artists with autism and to imagine that similar impulses may be at play in other precocious young artists less apparently engulfing narratives and visual undertakings. They all are as certainly documenting the places they have adopted or created in the many images that they draw with such great style and continuing interest as are the individuals who calculate grain prices or invent languages. At the same time, from our point of view, such world building in its broadest sense may be seen as a signpost expressed in art that marks and mirrors the road of daily experience for at least some precocious artists with autism.

8

The Queen of Makeup and the Clock Machine

Toward the end of the school year, the girls in Peter's second grade classroom were getting silly. In a moment of total hilarity they formed the Makeup Club and chose a president, eagerly making it clear to the disgruntled boys that only girls could belong. The irritated boys sought to retaliate, tossing off remarks about the worthlessness, stupidity, and vanity of females, thus inflaming the girls to greater extravagance and counterattack. Girls and boys alike were getting restless, ready for school to end and to turn to the serious business of play in the deep green summer of their nearly third-grade lives. Peter also felt the restlessness and he, too, was excited by the outbreak of teasing between boys and girls. As he always did when the emotional weather around him changed, he grabbed his markers and a piece of paper and began to draw. He worked carefully for some time, slowly rendering clearly outlined shapes and filling them in with solid, bold hues. Finished at last, he explained his drawing. "Look! It's the Queen of Makeup," he giggled, even weeks later. "She's the president of the Makeup Club!"

The Queen of Makeup is arresting in both its content and composition (see Figure 6.1). Though it is in Peter's usual solid, Disney-like animation style, the subject is a departure from all his previous imagery. It is a fictionalized picture of a girl in his class and an actual social event in the experience of the second grade, a reflection of the girl's activities glimpsed through Peter's inventive eyes. In the drawing, a muscular blonde in a tight blue dress with plunging neckline and modeling a flawless, sharp-edged page boy with split bangs strides toward the viewer, one hand dangling a rounded, wide-bristled hairbrush, the other, a substantial dryer with heavy cord and plug. Behind the plug a large black wall socket floats just below a blue bathtub with curved, capering feet. The tub, in turn, lies under a thick rod and cone, also blue, which make up a shower emitting two thin streams of water. Behind the queen's head drift two red, faceted trapezoids with heavy outlines, a glass stopper, and a perfume bottle pouring a sparkling stream of liquid onto the queen's shoulders. Though the style is familiar, the subject certainly is not; nor is it usual that Peter should create a drawing of his own social world without prompting or direct assignment from adults. The Makeup Queen pulls together in her assertive form Peter's cartoon-dominated past with actual current school events, for Peter knows the queen personally and took part in the rowdy classroom girl-boy confrontation. Then, after the struggle was over, he responded further to the second-grade battle of the sexes by forming a visual narrative of the incident with the bold shapes and bright colors on his paper.

Peter's drawing of the flamboyant Queen of Makeup, an image displaying his developing social integration and graphic skill, Jamie's earlier sweeping panoramic drawing of a beach cottage living room, and Katie's busy animals serve as examples of the complexities we struggled with even before we met the children themselves. Our earliest questions focused on the manner in which precocious young artists with autism make art: How are they able to draw in such a seemingly sophisticated, visually based, three-dimensional manner? How can they produce such drawings at an early age? Why do they seem so immediately and immensely pleased by the experience? And why do they repeat their efforts with such exceptional diligence? The second portion of our considerations are summed up by the figure of the striding queen herself, for she draws us into an area of inquiry that includes the interaction of image, memory, and language and their mutually supportive purposes in the task of creating meaning and sense. If our initial queries asked how precocious images by young artists come about, our following questions asked why, or for what purpose such images are created. Jamie, Katie, and Peter have illustrated the likely answers to both these series of questions in their art and have suggested that similar considerations may apply to the creations of other precocious young artists, too. Taken together or separately, the children's creations have displayed much of what we now suspect regarding the underlying function of art for artists with autism, particularly the creations of precocious young artists with this disorder.

In order to review and to clarify the possible answers to the questions we posed earlier regarding precocious art making and art itself, we will again turn to Jamie, Peter, Katie, and also to Mark, to two other young artists we have yet to meet, and to Nadia, the child with whom our inquiries began.

THE "HOW" OF PRECOCIOUS ART

Our initial considerations concerning the how of precocious perspectival art by young children with autism began with perhaps the best known of all such artists, Nadia, who, while a very young child, exhibited nearly all the characteristics of extraordinary early art making that have puzzled researchers and more casual viewers alike, since her earliest drawings were created in what has now become familiar to us as a typical precocious, perspectival style. Over the years, various explanations have been offered for such notable early abilities. These frequently include, among other related concerns: that the failure to develop language might be responsible for extraordinary graphic skill; and that perhaps such abilities appear only in connection with severe autistic disorder.

Our young exemplars, especially Jamie, however, have suggested the possibility of a different view. Though Jamie also began to draw at an early age with attention similar to Nadia's to lively linearity, foreshortening, and perspective in his architectural views, autos, and scenes of destruction, he possesses excellent language skills and is a member of an accelerated classroom. Certainly Jamie, and Peter and Katie in a less dramatic manner, seem to suggest that something other than lack of language or severe disability must lie at the heart of precocious art by young artists with autism. Even though their drawings share similar visual characteristics and a comparable early genesis with images created by Nadia, Jamie and Peter are not exceptionally developmentally or cognitively delayed, though certainly Katie is (and so, too, is Mark, who is certainly not precocious, but is in every way highly visual). Additionally, it is not the manner in which these young artists see that is in some way peculiar either, for even when they were very young their vision was to all accounts normal and none of the children currently wears glasses. The fact that the children have normal sight is significant, for vision is the most essential component of visually based drawings like Jamie's traffic tangles and buildings, Peter's Oz figures, Katie's creatures, and even Mark's gestural space images. It is clear from these images that Jamie, Peter, and Katie (and Mark, too), are using their eyes and brains to observe the world in a manner familiar to most of us and that they possess appropriately functioning eyes and visual systems.

The usual process of vision itself appears to provide a more satisfying explanation than disability for such precocious art. At the same time that ordinary vision helps to explain the mechanics or origin of early graphic skills, it appears that seeing also provides a sensible reason for precocious art's qualities, for there are marked similarities between vision's early image constructions and the visually based art of young artists with autism. It seems more likely, there-fore, that such drawing expertise is caused by something other than intellectual disability or unusual vision and may in fact be rooted in failure to develop social intelligence with an accompanying inability to amplify certain sociocultural constructs and skills. It is possible that this failure to develop these abilities lies at the heart of both the early creation of images and the accompanying connec-tion to unobscured visual processes.

This vision-based understanding of precocious art making by children with autism has implications for other artists, too, for it frees art from the consider-ation of language as its counterweight, impediment, and replacement, a skill that necessarily supplants the need for visual image making and that thereby relegates drawing and art to their most significant roles only in preliterate and/or early childhood development and cognition. Since so much of one's brain is devoted to visual processes, and since encountering visual patterns that reflect the constructs (we have also used the words "primitives" and "aesthetic primitives" here) of one's mind seem to produce pleasure, it is no surprise that young artists with autism find delight in, and are engrossed by, creating images as Nadia did earlier, and as Jamie, Peter, and Katie do now. Or, that in a less im-mediately obvious manner, children who arrange objects in rows or create pat-terns in some other manner likely do, too. At the sheer visual level, this ability to see and respond to arrangements of lines and shapes is a significant aspect of human cognition. It is one that must be present in almost all people who are able to see and one that forms, even at this most basic level, a link between the interior person and her exterior world. Additionally, this visually based under-standing of image making by young artists with autism suggests additional rea-sons besides pleasure for the response to such familiar forms, for as we have discovered, seeing and drawing are also valid means of creating meaning for these young artists, and simple narrative can be found in the repetition of shapes or colors just as surely as meaning can be located in the more complex graphic structures into which forms can be arranged in adult-created arts of all sorts. It is with this narrative, meaning-making quality of images that we finish both our answers and our stories as we meet Carl and his wire-filled box and discuss the why of art making.

THE "WHY" OF PRECOCIOUS ART

Years ago a boy with autism assembled a clock machine, a contrivance en-acting not only his preoccupations, but a story, a tale that engaged his peers and created a way for the boy to locate himself within the flow of his own life in the steady ". . . once . . . now . . . then . . ." of being and experience. Hugging his gadget to his chest as he stood in front of the class during show-and-tell, the boy became, however idiosyncratically, part of his classmates' lives at the same time they became part of his, as he told them a tale of a mouse and time, a story that remains today in the still remembered shape of the slight artist-storyteller clutching a description of his world. The boy's story, however, begins a bit earlier on the way to school, under his beloved umbrella on the streets of a leafy old suburb on the edge of a large city. Carl, a small child dressed all in green—pants, socks, shirt, and carrying an open green umbrella even though the day was sunny and fine—walked purposefully along the tree-shaded, quiet suburban street , touching particular spots on trees and fences as he always did, a shopping bag dangling from his hand. Later that day at school during show-and-tell in his third-grade classroom, the contents of the bag became the reason for Carl's telling and sharing, for as was often the case, he had brought his clock machine, a box filled with wires, lengths of tape, small pieces of wood, bright strands of heavy yarn, and bits of a large dismembered windup alarm clock, the leading character in his frequent school narratives, along with the ratty, hand-sized stuffed mouse that inhabited the lower righthand corner of the box. The invention was Carl's favorite construction, story, and fantasy world, the home of the mouse, and always an occasion for a long discourse on the interaction of clock parts and the battered gray inhabitant. This spring afternoon Carl spoke again to his classmates, his singsong voice seemingly moving forever into the lazy, chalk-dusted school sunlight. Finally, at the teacher's gently prompting, he returned his clock to the bag and walked to his desk as another child hurried eagerly to take his place, clutching the treasure that she, too, wanted to share with her classmates.

Why do children (and adults) with autism and those without create such contraptions or images and stories? Why do people make marks and constructions in a variety of ways in an endless number of substances, and how are visual thinking, the source of these marks and creations, and the genesis of narrative and meaning, related?

We have approached these problems from a variety of angles, listening to literal narratives and exploring abstract configurations that make up the art and personal stories of several artists' with autism. We have expanded our understanding of the word narrative or story, moving from an always literal, language-bound tale to the realization that narrative is the method people have of constituting meaning, which may lie almost holographically in the shapes, amount, doodles, arrangements, and structures created with the mark-making tools and many materials they possess. We have learned that though language may be linked to images in some ways, no one dreams only in words or arranges their world merely on the basis of language, and we have seen that our greatest pleasures and deepest fears usually present themselves in images and forms, in bright visible memories, not as strings of unadorned words or as text.

This multilayered, narrative-producing place of images in human cognition, memory, and meaning provides several new perspectives on the place of art in human experience as it suggests new perspectives on the startling early genesis and role of art for young artists with autism. At the same time, it provides an enlarged perspective on simple repetitive pattern-making activities in other, less graphically inclined children with autism, too. Art and creative imagery in this expanded perspective can be seen as major aspects of the means by which artists and many other visual thinkers constitute personal narrative meaning from their experiences, and art viewing can be understood to provide most observers a rich sense of shared human sentience and personal emotional depth as well as a satisfying, ordered repetition of some of the most intimate structures of their minds.

At the same time, art itself, in its role as an aspect of memory, as a mimetic device, and as a significant means of both expressing and creating meaning, can also be understood as a way to organize the flow of experience and cognitive functioning into orderly and sense-making narrative structures, the way Carl's clock provided meaning and sense for its creator. Carl's clock machine was a structural narrative made manifest, much like Jamie's architecture, electrical systems, and auto engines. It was Carl's personal story told in spatial relationships and three-dimensional interactions; the wire-filled box was his interior world made visible, his system for constructing and describing meaning. It can be understood to be the story he told himself and others about himself as he created solid personally satisfying emotional ground in his stressful disordered world.

A final story is instructive. In a large urban area in the upper Midwest, a small, dark-haired, middle-school boy with high-functioning autism spends his free time exploring structures he creates through mathematical means. Though his interest lies almost entirely in the world of numbers, colors also play a role in his complicated system, for colors have numerical equivalents that dictate their relationships to one another. This hue-related mathematical understanding is demonstrated on the surface of a hand-built cylinder vase he completed in art class. It is divided into small rectangles of repeated glaze colors based on his numerical systems (T. McCauley, personal communication, January 22, 1998). The vase's surface is reminiscent of the art of another artist with autism, Jessy Park, in her multihued painting of the facade of Duke University chapel, where colors play back and forth across its surface, balancing, matching, emphasizing, and describing various interactions and relationships in the geometric shapes of the building's exterior (Park, 1994). Though the boy's cylinder is a rather lumpy, beginner's affair unlike Jessy's elegant, careful art, we can still glimpse in its lopsided form a sense of what Park describes in her daughter's paintings when she writes, "The vision Jessy paints is not ours, but through her art we can share it, incandescent with the secrecy of her inner life, the hooded intensity of her smile" (Park, 1982, p. 303). Similarly, we can also share in the young boy's personal sense of order, in his world of meaning made clear in the shapes of mathematical relationships. These relationships are transformed into seeable structures that knit his interior and exterior world into a creation that grows from the complex relationship of his own personal meanings and creative abilities. The colored rectangles are thought made perceptible; they provide insight into the boy's world of sense making as well as a new perspective on our own.

Art, then, can be seen as our personal story as it comes to us, put down, as Fein (1993) pointed out, in identical human visual structures that spring up in or reverberate within everyone everywhere: colored rectangles or other simplified perceptual constructs, linear, wiry contraptions and complicated systems in which interactions are perceptible elements; buildings and cars whose forms are structures made seeable; skies and land masses whose relationships and complexities are as familiar and as part of our mental makeup as recognition of a human face; and all the other bright fierce shapes of our minds and lives, perceivable building blocks that are the basic stuff of the processes of seeing, language, and memory. Art relates our personal and social narratives in amounts and forms that are emphasized and ordered most simply in repetitions, and it is the description of our inner and outer worlds, painted, carved, scratched, or formed on a variety of surfaces or in endless types of materials, our memory's messenger as gay as a red zigzag, as emphatic as a striding, assertive queen, as complex as a clock machine. It is the discernible expression of the stories we all tell ourselves and wish to share with others as we make our way through the often difficult, frequently beautiful, always astonishing world that is common to us all.

Endpaper

What, one might wonder, is the importance of art for adolescents and older adults with autism who may or may not be retarded and who likely are not precocious artists? How can art making be of value in the flat, cold gray light of adult struggles with economic, domestic, and social existence for those people who are not outstanding artists like Stephen Wiltshire, Jessy Park, Richard Wawro, or exceptional designers like Temple Grandin, or who have not caught the eye of an eager sponsor? What is the point of early art making if eventually parental hopes and dreams, understandable as they are, are not fulfilled when a child grows up? Will the talk of narrative, of meaning, of the creation of a place to stand in the flow of time and experience, of connections with others, of making real fade as children become young adults and then middle-aged and older and their lives are likely lived out in group homes or assisted-living units and art recedes to a leisure activity? Where is the hope, value, and import of art then?

Three drawings and their creators—all of whom have cognitive disabilities and only one of whom was a precocious child artist and now is grown to adulthood—may provide examples and suggestions as a means to address these perturbing questions. The first drawing was created by a middle-school boy on the first day of a new school year. The second was done by a young woman in her twenties during art time in an activity center for adults with autism. The third image was carefully rendered by a man in his forties, a graduate of, and continuing participant in, a lifetime support program for people with autism. In the spaces between and among these people and their art—the middle schooler and his pencil drawing of a cat, the young woman and her looming squares, and the man and his Victorian dwelling—may lie answers to the questions posed regarding the value of art in the lives of people with autism who continue only casually to make art throughout their lives.

The first drawing was created in the upper Midwest by a middle-school boy in the first art class of the school year in a school for students with severe learning disabilities.

Seated with the other children in the art room, the boy, like his classmates, immediately set to work on the assignment, a pencil drawing of his family as an introduction to fellow students and the teacher. After he had made several marks, however, it became clear that the boy had other ideas, for he began to draw a simple single form that seemed not at all human, and no amount of coaxing could dissuade him from it. First, in the upper-left quarter of his large sheet of newsprint he drew a small germ form with a misshaped rectangular body topped by a crude circular head. It was a "cat," he said, not his human family. He formed the eyes and mouth with small empty circles. The head, surmounted by a series of scribbles, seemed to wear a mortarboard at a rakish angle that nearly obscured the half-dozen loose marks that might be ears, an extra hat, or nothing at all. The cat's legs and tail were mere hints—five nearly invisible short lines, more like cilia than other, more substantial appendages. Next, the boy traced a drafting triangle over the animal, bisecting the beast at the waist with one of the two short sides of the template. The triangle's other side slanted over the cat's head, a shed roof of thick, dark marks. Clearly charmed by the plastic instrument, the boy finally covered most of the remaining paper with identical triangle forms—single and multiple outlines piled on top of one another. Finally, as if to hold these tracing down, the boy then outlined two larger triangle templates on top of the thick heap of smaller forms at the bottom of the paper. Nearly obliterated by this barrage of triangles, a centrally placed, lumpy circle barely survived under the dense pile while its twin clung to the left edge of the paper near the cat. The boy completed his image with pencil dots that formed an overall skrim of whack marks, made as he repeatedly struck his pencil on the paper, likely enjoying the sound as well as the vigorous marks he made (C. Ambler, personal communication, July 6, 1999).

Perhaps finding satisfaction in repetition and control, or in the creation of lines and edges themselves low level aesthetic primitives and "powerful triggers of neural activity low down in the cortical visual pathways in primary visual cortex" (Latto, 1995, p. 86), or taking pleasure in the circles and triangles that have similar roles as edges and lines as geometric aesthetic primitives, or simply in creating an image that includes a cat as part of a vigorous linear composition that links his past (the cat) to his present (the art room, drawing, and triangles), the boy created, at least for that moment, pleasure for himself as well as a visible bridge to the world of teacher, classmates, and school. No matter how rickety and idiosyncratic the cat drawing on its own, like the art of the young artists we encountered earlier, it is not a useless undertaking, for it ties the boy to the social world of school and home with satisfying visual threads of his own devising.

The second image was created in the same day care center for adults with autism where the young man with the red crayon also spends time. Its creator, a young woman, is also a regular participant in the center's program. The drawing, a large red and green watercolor, is of particular interest because of the contrast between her behavior while creating it and her activities while not engaged in making art. A brief description of both her behavior and art making will add significantly to our understanding.

Dressed in jeans and a short-sleeved plaid shirt, her light brown, curly hair brushing her shoulders, the young woman ceaselessly, noiselessly paces the center's new short-napped carpeting, not speaking, veering silently from one person to the next in an attempt to touch them on whatever portion of their anatomy she is most easily able to poke as she cruises past. Her touch is gentle, a trailing of a finger, a gentle prod, always from behind or from an direction that affords her an unseen angle of approach to her quarry and a quick escape. Though not hurtful, her habit of touching has gotten her in difficulty in public places on several occasions, for she touches anyone anywhere as long as she can make a rapid getaway. Recently in a McDonald's, for example, as she silently glided through the lines, she had run her finger along a young man's backside as he waited to place his order. The man had became angry, and the center workers had a difficult time explaining her behavior to his satisfaction. Since that event, everyone had become especially eager to extinguish her touching to avoid further trouble, but she is fast, focused, and looking for opportunities, and it is difficult to shift her attention elsewhere.

It is at this point that her drawing enters the story, for the young woman's engagement during art time with her large pencil image of two tiny human figures squashed against opposite sides of her paper kept her involved first with pencil and watercolors for a full forty minutes. During that time, she was not lying in wait to touch anyone as she softly smiled over her drawing. She was busy with her figures' stick arms and legs, round smiling heads, and rectangular, blocky bodies and the two enormous rectangles that seemed to press them to the paper's edges. Surely she was involved in creating a scene of some sort, for the rectangles that formed her simple central shapes were similar to the very earliest houses drawn by four- and five-year-old children; and her beaming figures were carefully and intentionally placed on either side of the larger forms on a ground line implied by the bottom of the paper, just as young children also use the paper's lower edge as a built-in compositional element. The young woman's drawing is in some ways like the boy's cat image, for not only did she create a familiar pattern of arresting verticals and horizontals, but she also repeated in the round heads, rectangular bodies, and huge central rectangular forms familiar satisfying aesthetic primitives—shapes utilized by the visual processes to describe the characteristics of the world we all see. At the same time that the young woman's drawing described these basic pleasing aesthetic shapes, however, it also created a connection between her internal and external life in terms that engage her so entirely that her usual preoccupation with touching others—even as they brushed past her in the cramped art room—was pushed aside by the emerging shapes of two humans and perhaps a house.

The third and last image was created by a forty-seven-year-old man, Luke, whose autism was diagnosed between the ages of four and five by Leo Kanner, one of the two people who recognized, described, and named the condition of autism. A precocious artist from the time he was four, Luke's life story illustrates in many ways the spectrum of treatment of people with autism in the United States at least, for not only was he diagnosis by Kanner, but he was also the longest term-student in Bruno Bettleheim's Orthogenic School at the University of Chicago, having been a resident for sixteen years. Currently, however, Luke lives semi-independently with another adult in an apartment overseen by Chapel Haven, a program for people with autism from which he graduated years ago, and he continues to take an active part in the social activities provided by their social services. He also is employed bagging groceries in a nearby supermarket.

It is to Luke's art that we finally turn, for it is his engagement with the qualities of the visible world of structure and line that has provided a continuing subject for his imagery throughout his life and a significant indication of the preoccupations and perspectives that he shares with his younger sister, a professional artist.

Luke's engagement with the qualities of the visible world began even before he started to draw, for when he was three years old, he began using Tinker Toys to create elaborate architectural constructions emphasizing the linear composition of forms and the rich variety of spatial relationships that they describe. After his initial exploration of literal structure in the shape of toys, Luke soon moved to the use of pencil, watercolor, and straight-edge ruler, rendering complicated images of maps, fantasy college towns, architecture and utilizing what his sister refers to as his "intuitive perspective." (L. Hogin, personal communication, February 8, 2000).

A recent watercolor, a careful, two-point perspectival view of a large Victorian house set back from the road titled "The Institution Between Route 336 and 678" serves as a good example of Luke's more current work at the same time it describes several of his lifelong interests and drawing preoccupations. The image includes highway signs and labels. One sign reads "Copeland County NYS" and the other, "Kilometer's, Seegers 5, Senar Ridge 4, Jail'sport 8." It also includes a lavish use of several bright watercolor hues to enrich the entire image; a focus on architecture; and a visually based, perspectival, structurally focused, linear image. At the same time, it contains an indication of his continuing concern with institutionalization, a worry developed, his sister believes, during his long difficult stay at the Orthogenic Clinic in Chicago.

Luke's image, similar in many ways to the drawings of Stephen Wiltshire and Jamie at first glance, is especially focused on the intricacies of built space, of visual structure made manifest in brick, stone, and cement, and of details of facades, with line as the most important element in the determination of both shape and space. Color, as is true with Stephen's and Jamie's art, is a final additive element. One encounters not only the same qualities in Luke's drawing that can be seen in these other architecturally inclined artists with autism, but also the same visually based, deeply structural, energetic engagement with the seeable world, and by implication, a suggestion as to the portion of visual processes that considers them.

Perhaps these final three people in their diverse and unexotic lives (no Disney artists here, nor Wawro-like professionals) suggest in their drawings the most important aspects of art for the majority of people with autism. They repeat in a manner that is clearly independent of the extraordinary, precocious, or unusual the fact that art is, even for the unextraordinary art maker with autism, a useful means of expressing their interior selves, of sharing with others the very substance of their minds as they relate a tale of their own creating, and finally, of visibly forming enduring links with other people in the common human language of lines and forms.

These accomplishments are at least as important to a life as any other form of meaning-making activity, for they, too, enable one person to reach out beyond herself to another individual or to the entire world with some of the deepest, most especially human qualities of her mind.

References

Adams, R., Victor, M., & Ropper, A. (1997). *Principles of neurology* (sixth ed.). New York: McGraw-Hill.

Alland, A. (1983). *Playing with form.* New York: Columbia University Press.

Axelrod, J. (1999). Catecholamines. In G. Edleman & B. Smith (Eds.), *Encyclopedia of Neuroscience.* Amsterdam: Elsevier. 316–318.

Bachelard, G. (1994). *The poetics of space.* Boston: Beacon.

Bahn, P. (1998). *Prehistoric art.* Cambridge, England: Cambridge University Press.

Baron-Cohen, S. (1995). *Mindblindness: An essay on autism and theory of mind.* Cambridge, MA: MIT Press.

Becker, G. (1997). *Disrupted lives: How people create meaning in a chaotic world.* Berkeley: University of California Press.

Bellah, R., Madsen, R., Sullivan, W., Swindler, A., & Tipton, S. (1985). *Habits of the heart: Individualism and commitment in American life.* New York: Harper and Row.

Breen, K. (1999). Art lifts curtain on child's world. *Press and Sun Republic.* Retrieved July 2, 1999 from the World Wide Web: www.jonathanlerman.com/about

Bruner, J. (1986). *Actual minds, possible worlds.* Cambridge, MA: Harvard University Press.

Büchel, C., Price, C., & Friston, K. (1998). A multimodal language region in the ventral visual pathway. *Nature, 394* (6690), 274–277.

Burd, L., Severud, R., Kerbeshian, J., & Klug, M. (1999). Prenatal and perinatal risk factors for autism. *Journal of Perinatal Medicine, 27* (6), 441–450.

Burr, D., Morrone, M., & Ross, J. (1994). Selective suppression of the magnocellular visual pathway during saccadic eye movements. *Nature, 371* (6497), 511–513.

Cipolotti, L., Robinson, G., Blair, J., & Frith, U. (1999). Fractionation of visual memory: Evidence from a case with multiple neurodevelopmental impairments. *Neuropsychologia, 37,* 455–465.

Conway, M. (1990). *Autobiographical memory.* Philadelphia: Open University Press.

Cowey, A. (1995). Blindsight is real sight. *Nature, 377* (6547), 290–291.

Crick, F. (1995). Are we aware of neural activity in the primary visual cortex? *Nature, 375* (6527), 121–123.

Damasio, A. (1995). Knowing how, knowing where. *Nature, 357* (6527), 106–107.

Davis, J. (1998). Drawing's demise: U-shaped graphic development in graphic symbolization. *Studies in Art Education, 38* (3), 132–157.

Engel, S. (1995). *The stories children tell.* New York: W. H. Freeman.

Fein, S. (1993). *First drawings.* Pleasant Hill, CA: Exelrod.

Folstein, S., Bisson, E., Santangelo, S., & Piven, J. (1998). Finding specific genes that cause autism: A combination of approaches will be needed to maximize power. *Journal of Autism and Developmental Disorder, 28* (5), 439–445.

Frith, U. (1995). *Autism: Explaining the enigma.* Oxford, England: Blackwell.

Frith, U. (1994). *Autism and Asperger syndrome.* New York: Cambridge University Press.

Frith, U. & Happé, F. (1994). Autism: Beyond the "theory of mind." *Cognition, 50,* 115–132.

Gardner, H., & Winner, E. (1982). First intimations of artistry. In S. Strauss (Ed.), *U-shaped behavioral growth.* New York: Academic.

Ghaziuddin, M., & Burmeister, M. (1999). Deletion of chromosome 2 q37 and autism: A distinct subtype? *Journal of Autism and Developmental Disorders, 29* (3), 259–263.

Gillberg, C. (1998). Chromosomal disorders and autism. *Journal of Autism and Developmental Disorders, 28* (5), 415–425.

Grandin, T. (1995a). How people with autism think. In E. Schopler & G. Mesibov (Eds.), *Learning and cognition in autism.* New York: Plenum. 137–155.

Grandin, T. (1995b). *Thinking in pictures.* New York: Doubleday.

Grandin, T. (1992). An inside view of autism. In E. Schopler & G. Mesibov (Eds.), *High functioning individuals with autism.* New York: Plenum. 105–125.

Gross, J., & Hayne, H. (1998). Drawing facilitates children's verbal reports of emotionally laden events. *Journal of Experimental Psychology: Applied, 4* (2), 163–179.

Hamkalo, B. (1991). Chromosomes. In R. Dulbecco (Ed.), vol. 2. *Encyclopedia of Human Biology.* New York: Academic. 465–474.

Happé, F. (1995). *Autism.* Cambridge, MA. Harvard University Press.

Hoffman, D. (1998). *Visual intelligence.* New York: W. W. Norton.

Hollander, E., DelGiudice-Asch, G., Simon, L., Schmeidler, J., Cartwright, C., DeCaria, C., Kwon, J., Cunningham-Rundles, C., Chapman, F., & Zabriskie, J. (1999). B lymphocyte antigen D8/17 and repetitive behaviors in autism. *The American Journal of Psychiatry, 156* (2), 317–320.

Hubbard, R. (1989). *Authors of pictures, draughtsmen of words.* Portsmouth, NH: Heinemann.

Humphreys, G. (1995). Acting without "seeing." *Nature, 374* (6525), 763–764.

Ingram, J. L., Stodgell, C. J., Hyman, S. L., Figlewicz, D. A., Weitkamp, L. R., & Rodier, P. (2000). Discovery of allelic varients of HOXA1 and HOXB1:

Genetic susceptibility to autism spectrum disorders. *Teratology, 62* (6), 393–405.

Insel, T., O'Brien, D., & Leckman, J. (1999). Oxytocin, vasopressin, and autism: Is there a connection? *Biological Psychiatry, 45* (2), 145–157.

Kass, J. (1995). Vision without awareness. *Nature, 373* (6511), 195.

Kellman, J. (1999a). Drawing with Peter: Autobiography, narrative, and the art of a child with autism. *Studies in Art Education, 40* (3), 258–274.

Kellman, J. (1999b). Narrative and the art of two children with autism. *Visual Art Research, 24* (2), 38–48.

Kellman, J. (1998). Ice Age vision: Autism and vision, how we see and how we draw. *Studies in Art Education, 39* (2), 117–131.

Kellman, J. (1996). Making sense of seeing: Autism and David Marr. *Visual Arts Research, 22* (2), 76–89.

Kellman, J. (1995). Harvey shows the way: Narrative in children's art. *Art Education, 48* (2), 18–22.

Kellman, J. (1991). *Weaving huipiles: Narratives of three Maya women.* Unpublished doctoral dissertation, The University of Iowa, Iowa City.

Kellogg, R. (1970). *Analyzing children's art.* Palo Alto, CA: Mayfield.

Kosslyn, S., Thompson, W., Kim, I., & Alpert, N. (1995). Topographical representations of mental images in primary visual cortex. *Nature, 378* (6556), 496.

Langer, S. (1982). *Philosophy in a new key.* Cambridge, MA: Harvard University Press.

Langer, S. (1953). *Feeling and form.* New York: Charles Scribner.

Latto, R. (1995). The brain of the beholder. In R. Gregory, J. Harris, P. Heard, & D. Rose (Eds.), *The artful eye.* New York: Oxford University Press.

Lauritsen, M., Mors, O., Mortensen, P., & Ewald, H. (1999). Infantile autism and associated autosomal chromosome abnormalities: A register-based study and literature survey. *Journal of Child Psychology and Psychiatry, 40* (3), 335–345.

London, P. (1997, April). The most important thing is to believe in one's own self and what one does. Paper presented at the meeting of the National Art Education Association Conference, New Orleans, LA.

Lopez, B. (1990). *Crow and Weasel.* San Francisco: North Point.

Lopez, B. (1981). *Winter count.* New York: Scribners.

Lowenfeld, V., & Brittain, W. L. (1987). *Creative and mental growth.* New York: Macmillian.

Maestrini, E., Marlow, A., Weeks, D., & Monaco, A. (1998). Molecular genetic investigations of autism. *Journal of Autism and Developmental Disorders, 28* (5), 427–437.

Marr, D. (1982). *Vision, a computational investigation into the human representation and processing of visual information.* New York: W. H. Freeman.

Marshall, J., & Halligan, P. (1995). Seeing the forest but only half the trees. *Nature, 373* (6514), 521–523.

Merritt's Textbook of Neurology. (1995). L. Rowland. (Ed.) Baltimore: Williams and Wilkins.

Mithen, S. (1996). *The prehistory of the mind, the cognitive origins of art, religion and science.* New York: Thames and Hudson.

Mottron, L., Burack, J., Stauder, J., & Robaey, P. (1999). Perceptual processing among high-functioning persons with autism. *Journal of Child Psychology and Psychiatry, 40* (2), 203–211.

Nolte, J. (1999). *The human brain.* St. Louis, MO: Mosby.

Nolte, J., & Angevine Jr., J. (1995). *The human brain in photographs and diagrams.* St. Louis, MO: Mosby.

Oxford Dictionary of Biochemistry and Molecular Biology. (2000). A. D. Smith (Ed.). London: Oxford University Press.

Paley, V. (1990). *The boy who would be a helicopter.* Cambridge, MA: Harvard University Press.

Pariser, D., & van den Berg, A. (1997). The mind of the beholder: some provisional doubts about the U-curved aesthetic development thesis. *Studies in Art Education, 38* (3), 159–178.

Park, C. (1994). Autism into art: A handicap transformed. In E. Schopler & G. Mesibov (Eds.), *High functioning individuals with autism.* New York: Plenum.

Park, C. (1982). *The siege.* Boston: Little Brown.

Park, D. & Youderian, P. (1974). Light and number: Ordering principles in the world of an autistic child. *Journal of Autism and Childhood Schizophrenia, 4* (4), 313–323.

Piven, J., Arndt, S., Bailey, J., Havercamp, S., Andreasen, N., & Palmer, P. (1995). An MRI study of brain size in autism. *American Journal of Psychiatry, 152* (8), 1145–1149.

Plaisted, K., O'Riordan, M., & Baron-Cohen, S. (1998a). Enhanced discrimination of novel, highly similar stimuli by adults with autism during a perceptual learning task. *Journal of Child Psychology and Psychiatry, 39* (5), 765–775.

Plaisted, K., O'Riordan, M., & Baron-Cohen, S. (1998b). Enhanced visual search for a conjunctive target in autism: A research note. *Journal of Child Psychology and Psychiatry, 39* (5), 777–783.

Potgieter, S., & Fryns, J. (1999). The neurobiology of autism. *Genetic Counseling, 10* (2), 117–122.

Researcher unravels miswiring in the schizophrenic brain. (2000). *The University of Iowa Spectator, 33* (3), 11.

Rodier, P. (2000). The early origins of autism. *Scientific American, 282,* (2) 56–63.

Rutter, M. (1999). Autism: Two-way Interplay between research and clinical work. *Journal of Child Psychology and Psychiatry, 40* (2), 169–188.

Sacks, O. (1995). *An anthropologist on Mars.* New York: Alfred A. Knopf.

Sacks, O. (1985). *The man who mistook his wife for a hat and other clinical tales.* New York: Quality Paperbacks.

Salmon, B., Hallmayer, J., Rogers, T., Kalaydjieva, L., Petersen, P.B., Nicholas, P., Pingree, C., McMahon, W., Spiker, D., Lotspeich, L., Kraemer, H., McCague, P., Dimiceli, S., Nouri, N., Pitts, T., Yang, J., Hinds, D., Meyers, R.M., & Risch, N. (1999). Absence of linkage and linkage disequalibrium to chromosome 15q11-q13 markers in 139 multiplex families with autism. *American Journal of Medical Genetics, 88* (5), 551–556.

Schutz, A. (1970). *On phenomenology and social relations.* H. Wagner (Ed.). Chicago: The University of Chicago Press.

Selfe, L. (1977). *Nadia.* London: Academic.

Shahn, B. (1985). *The shape of content*. Cambridge, MA: Harvard University Press.

Strauss, S. (1982). *U-shaped behavioral growth*. New York: Academic.

Swettenham, J., Baron-Cohen, S., Charman, T., Cox, A., Baird, G., Drew, A., Rees, L., & Wheelwright, S. (1998). The frequency and distribution of spontaneous attention shifts between social and nonsocial stimuli in autistic, typically developing, and nonautistic developmentally delayed infants. *Journal of Child Psychology and Psychiatry, 39* (5), 747–753.

Tasman, A., Kay, J., & Lieberman, J. (Eds.) (1997). Psychiatry. Philadelphia: W.B. Saunders. Retrieved May 31, 2000, from the World Wide Web: http://home.mdconsult.com/das/book/body/15027249/885/105.html

Taylor, D. (1995a). *Katie*. Unpublished manuscript.

Taylor, D. (1995b). *Student profile*. Unpublished manuscript.

Treffert, D. (1989). *Extraordinary people*. New York: Harper & Row.

Trottier, G., Srivastava, L., & Walker, C. (1998). Etiology of infantile autism: A review of recent advances in genetic and neurobiological research. *Journal of Psychiatry and Neuroscience, 24* (2), 103–115.

Wawro, M. (Producer, Director). (1989). *A real rainman, a portrait of an autistic savant* [Film]. Plymouth, MN: Scimitar Entertainment.

Webster's New Twentieth-Century Dictionary. (1979). J. McKechnie. (Ed.) New York: Simon and Schuster.

Williams, K. (1995). Understanding students with Asperger syndrome. *Focus on Autistic Behavior, 10* (2). Retrieved July 9, 1999, from the World Wide Web: http://www.udel.edu/bkirby/asperger/karen_williams_guidelines.html

Williams, M. (1922, 1991). *The velveteen rabbit*. New York: Doubleday.

Wiltshire, S. (1991). *Floating cities*. New York: Summit Books.

Wiltshire, S. (1989). *Cities*. London: J. M. Dent.

Wiltshire, S. (1987). *Drawings*. London: J. M. Dent.

Wing, L. (1994). *The relationship between Asperger's Syndrome and Kanner's autism*. In *Autism and Asperger Syndrome*. U. Frith (Ed.). New York: Cambridge University Press. 93–121.

Zurmuehlen, M. (1991). Stories that fill the center. *Art Education, 44* (6), 6–11.

Zurmuehlen, M. (1990). *Studio art: Praxis, symbol, presence*. Reston, VA: National Art Education Association.

Zurmuehlen, M. (1987). Storytelling for the art classroom. *Texas Trends In Art Education*. (Annual publication of the Texas Art Education Association, Austin, Texas)

Zurmuehlen, M. (1986). Reflecting on the ordinary: Interpretation as transformation of experience. *Art Education*. July, 33–36.

Zurmuehlen, M. (1983). From as metaphor: A comparison of aesthetic structure in young children's pictures and drawings. *Studies in Art Education, 24* (2), 111–117.

Zurmuehlen, M. (1981). How art gives meaning to experience. *Art Education*. July, 24–26.

Index

About the Author

JULIA KELLMAN is Assistant Professor of Art Education, School of Art and Design, University of Illinois at Urbana-Champaign.